I0168481

Ballycurragh to Tasmania 1649 – 1868

Volume One

The Grey Family and Innes Clan

Illustrated by Richard Chuck

Contributions by Paddy Murray and Paddy Heaney (Ireland) Jim Everett-puralia meenamatta

Written and edited by Kate Dougharty and Ian Broinowski

Self Published

© Broinowski Ian 2018 48 Colville St Battery Point Hobart 7004 ibroinow-ski@netspace.net.au

This book is copyright however it may be reproduced freely although full acknowledg- ment is required

The information contained in this book is to the best of the authors' and publisher's knowledge true and correct. Every effort has been made to ensure its accuracy, but the authors and publisher do not accept responsibility for any loss, injury or damage arising from such information.

ISBN 9780992373566

Dedication

This book is dedicated to
Paddy Murray and his beloved Roscomroe
01/05/1939 – 30/07/2018

Contents

Acknowledgements (from Kate Dougharty 1954)

I wish to thank all those dear friends who have given me sympathetic encourage ment, especially Mrs. Bruce Walker, who typed the manuscript and attended to all the necessary business part, Mr. Karl von Stieglitz for his charming preface and Doctor Gol- lan for his interest. The original text was wholly set up and printed by the Telegraph Printery Pty. Ltd., 63 Charles Street, Launceston, Tasmania.

Foreword

Most of us, if we had been bed-ridden in hospital for eight years, not even able to turn over unassisted and often wracked by cruel arthritic pains, would feel too sorry for ourselves to make any effort.

Not so, however, is the compiler of this true family record, Miss Kate Dougharty, who has fought back every inch of the way, as her fighting Scottish ancestors would have done.

Not content with writing several amusing talks about hospital life for the A.B.C., she has now put together the story of her pioneer ancestors in Tasmania.

In doing this, she has used the letters they wrote—you should see them, all brown with age and carefully tied up with pieces of ribbon into little parcels— and her excellent memory which vividly recorded the old tales of Van Diemen's Land and its people, she had been told as a child. Those who read this book will know, too, that her description of the dresses worn in the old days is exactly correct, for she has made a study of the subject and has a cupboard full of garments at home, where she used to keep them aired and protected as they had always been kept

since her people wore them.

Mrs. Bruce (Mary) Walker, whose voice is often heard on national stations, has spared time in her busy life on the land, with a husband and children to look after into the bargain, to help Miss Dougharty, for she typed the manuscript and gave encouragement generously all the way through.

May this little book meet with the great success it deserves and may Miss Dougharty find some more letters in her old desk to use in writing another volume.

(Sgd.) K. K. VON STIEGLITZ, "Andora," Evandale.

Preface

We touch history through the tips of our fingers. We hold faded and folded letters from the past, tracing our fingers along the lines of scrawl both across the page and overlapped from top to bottom. We feel the red and broken seal or untie and retie the ribbon around documents of the past. Our touch reaches theirs, our far distant family who wrote with feather pen and ink in a world closer to Jane Austen than our own. As children we played with objects from the past, opened jars and explored our mother's jewelry box so full of magic and mystery. We touched and smelt musty muffs, shawls and dresses worn at balls with candle light and immersed in a long for- gotten culture of British customs so alien to the Van Diemen's Land bush, shrubs and wildlife just beyond the windows.

We lived with tales and stories familiar to our parents, of people we never knew or met briefly as their lives faded and ours had just begun. We touched them and they us. As we grew our children too learned of the folk lore of their family but to a lesser extent, as each generation is lost just a little more to the next until people become a name only, a birth or death notice in the paper, devoid of life or character. They have vanished just as we will as further generations take over the trinkets of the past.

Kate Hamilton Dougharty (Katie) though did more. She held in her hands letters, diaries, books and most of all childhood tales from her ex- tensive family and began to write. The result was her book, *A Story of a Pioneer Family in Van Diemen's Land* published almost as she died and revealing her passion and desire to pass on all she knew to unknown generations to come.

Some things we touch are lost in our lives as fingers become numb with indifference or neglect. Katie's book is one of those possessions as- sociated with a past generation which I grew up with, in book shelves of different houses throughout my lifetime, occasionally to be flicked through, read a little and returned to collect dust or to be packed up and moved to another location. Time makes our touch less acute and dampens our senses.

Written by Kate Dougharty late in her life and during an extended stay in hospital for arthritis, surrounded by mementos and family folklore she drew together the many stories which had been part of her childhood and ethos. She would have known well several of the characters in the book who were her aunts Catherine, Henrietta and her grandmother Lysbeth.

Her writing reflects such sentiment and is a genre perhaps unfamiliar to current readers with a fabled, sometimes overly sentimental, flair. How- ever it does portray the events, both joyous and poignant, very much from a woman's perspective, which is unusual in historical writing of this era. This in itself makes it a worthwhile read, it is insightful, about real people and includes glimpses of everyday life of the girls growing up in Avoca, and their contemporaries in early Van Diemen's Land.

Perhaps though the best way to appreciate her work is to view it as scenes of a play. The characters were real, their being continuous throughout the years but occasionally we are allowed into a small part of their lives as they reveal their thoughts, times of adventure, happiness, sadness and changes beyond their control which influence existence. As with any theatre there are many factors behind the scenes which make it all possible and are interesting in their own right. The last section delves into the world beyond the play and provides a collage of facts, thoughts and some analysis of Katie's presentation.

A Gray Family Note Book beginning at the time of Cromwell's inva- sion of Ireland in 1649 with Lt Colonel John Gray is used as the basis for some of the additional research into this book and is referenced with the letters (FNB). The note book contains material collected by three family members over two centuries: Basil Gray, in the 18th Century, May Anderson 19th and Kate Dougharty in the 20th.

Sometimes though it takes a stranger to stretch out and touch something to make us realise what we have lost. Paul Tapp is just such a person who held this little book in his hands with obvious delight as he became engrossed in a long forgotten world so delightfully presented by Kate Hamilton Dougharty, my Great Aunt. My thanks to Paul Tapp for helping me to rediscover my family in such an insightful and imaginative manner. I would like to add special thanks to Frank Murray, Geoff Ayling, John Innes, Prue and Frank O'Connor and to Annie Rushton who has been a constant enthusiast in this project with meticulous editing and her open feedback. Finally to Dr Terry Whitebeach for providing a fresh perspective and critical analysis leading to a much more readable and enticing presentation.

My very special thanks must go to Paddy Murray and Paddy Heaney both well known local historians and authors from Offaly (Kings County) in Ireland whose passion for storytelling and the history of their beloved Roscomroe and surrounding towns flowed through to their interest and research to this book. With their help, we were able to uncover many intriguing aspects to the family and their lives in before their journey to VDL in the 1820's. Sadly though Paddy Murray passed away a few days before he was to receive the book.

Richard Chuck too deserves a special mention for his illustrations which perfectly match the era in which Kate was writing. I am sure she would have approved!

Synchronicity too played a small but crucial role when, by chance, I heard Jim Everett, puralia meenamatta, read his poem, *On the road with Buck* at the Tasmanian Writer's Festival. It was a powerful cry of loss and grief associated with the Fingal Valley and one intimately intertwined with this story: it too needed to be told.

Finally, book uses both Gray and Grey. It appears that Humphrey's father used Grey and hence it continued down his line while his cousins, William and James used Gray.

I hope you enjoy their story, Dr Ian Broinowski

.

STORY OF A PIONEER FAMILY

Kate Hamilton Dougharty 2 May 1879 -24 May 1954

Offaly (Kings) County

Dublin

Roscomroe

Letitia left Cove of

6

Introduction

This is an attempt to write the true history of my pioneer forebears. There were a great number of cultured, educated white settlers here in 1828. Their social life conformed as far as climate and their unexplored country would allow, to the life they had led in the "Old Country."

It has always seemed to me that in the pioneer books I have read, there has been too much dwelling on the convict question, so I have tried not to do that. Roscomroe, King's County, also Garry Castle, Galway, were the names of their original homes. Humphrey's home is called Eastbourne, and it still belongs to the family. I have a painting of the original house which was unfortunately burnt through the carelessness of a tenant. The house taking its place was built by an insurance company without the supervision of the family, and it is not as nice or as well planned. A tenant occupies it at present.

Grayfort and Rockford still exist, with the private burial ground but are absorbed into the Benham estate. I have a map showing the owners of the various grants in the district and have used these names in speaking of the dinner party guests. There were many inter-marriages amongst them.

I have Margaret Grey's diary of 1832, which speaks of the settlers who came and went in their home. In the incidents of taking wine, "the chairs and tables," and the Governor's visit, also the young settler's proposal, the wording is exactly the same as that used by my great-aunt, Catherine Grey, who told me of them.

I have the betrothal ring given to Catherine and worn by her all her life.

The table silver, manufactured in 1801 to celebrate the Union, still be- longs to us, because the Greys, glad of the event, hoped to hand it down to their descendants and used it only for weddings, parties and special occasions.

My dates are correct. It has taken me two years to be sure of their accuracy.

I had plenty of time to re- member the stories which were

Fire at Eastbourne, Near Avoca, Launceston

FIRE AT EASTBOURNE, NEAR AVOCA.—In our issue of Tuesday we mentioned the destruction of the family dwelling on this property ; we have since learned the following particulars :—The family were at breakfast on the morning of Sunday last. It was known that the chimney was on fire, but, as is often the case in the country, this was not thought much of, and it was only when the servant reported that smoke was coming through the roof that danger was anticipated. Then a wet bag was put over the blazing chimney's top ; but it is supposed that some of the mortar had in the course of years separated from it, and allowed the fire to reach the ceiling joists or roof, and in less than half an hour the whole of the wood-work was destroyed. The walls being of brick, and of unusual thickness, are apparantly not much injured ; but they are the only remains of a home well-known in the Avoca district, and from which at one time much hospitality was wont to flow. The building was erected by the late Mr Humphrey, Gray, and at the time of its destruction was occupied by Mr Hewitt, who is a severe sufferer, as stores, bedroom furniture, and indeed all that was in the second and upper floor was lost, and he had not taken the precaution to insure. Miss Gray was more prudent, but it is doubtful if her policy will cover her loss.

Launceston Examiner 1880, June 4, p. 3.

told me by my mother and great aunt. These are sup- ported by all the letters I hold. The incidents are not imaginary. It has been an interest and amusement to try to write them all out. All the letters are ex- act copiesof the originals in my possession—from the wreck onwards. I also have the little wedding dress and even Frederick's socks, waistcoat and nightcap. "*The Historical Account of the House of Innes*," from which I have quoted, was given to my grandfather, F. M. Innes, by his brother Francis in 1854. I have it now. It was printed for the family alone, in 1821 and cannot be bought.*

KATE HAMILTON DOUGHARTY,
St. Luke's Hospital, Launceston 1953

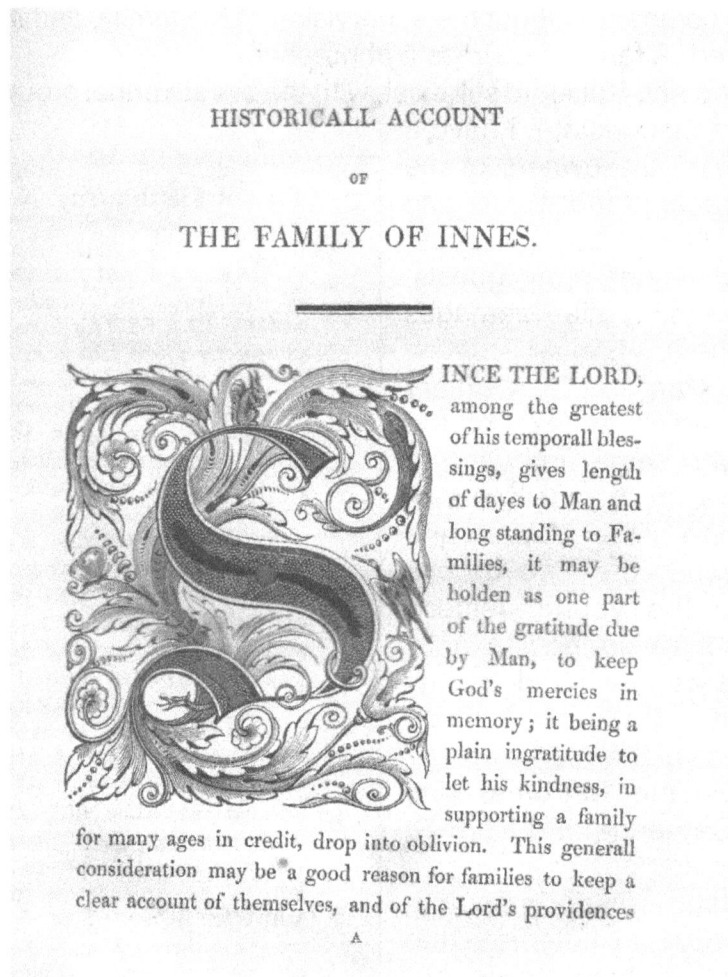

HISTORICALL ACCOUNT

OF

THE FAMILY OF INNES.

INCE THE LORD, among the greatest of his temporall blessings, gives length of dayes to Man and long standing to Families, it may be holden as one part of the gratitude due by Man, to keep God's mercies in memory; it being a plain ingratitude to let his kindness, in supporting a family for many ages in credit, drop into oblivion. This generall consideration may be a good reason for families to keep a clear account of themselves, and of the Lord's providences

A

Figure 1 Page on of Historicall Account of the Family of Innes

*Thanks to the quirkiness of the internet the 'old Innes history' book by Forbes Duncan *"Historical Account of the Origine and Succession of the Family of Innes"* 1820 Edinburgh Kessinger is now available online from Legacy Reprint.

AVOCA, TASMANIA IN 1838.
Before the church was built and with the bridge under construction.

Figure 2 Photograph - Sketch of Avoca, Launceston, from "EARLY VAN DIEMAN'S LAND 1835-1860 Sketches" by Emma Von Stieglitz

Figure 4 Roscomroe Medieval Church - Richard Chuck 2017

Gray Family Tree - William and James

Richard MD = Anne Kingsley b1760 d 25/4/1837 lived at Birr (Parsonstown), Kings Co.

* William 14 Mar 1793 - 10 March 1848 = Eleanor Toler Kingsley 1790 - 28/12/1869

James d 18/5/1849 = Mary Legge 1802 - 23 Oct 1865

Richard 1823 in Ireland - 28 Nov 1839 aged 16 Avoca; William Kingsley Gray born in Ireland d 10/1/1866 Bungrutrong NSW; Humphrey Arthur 1827 in VDL - 15/4/1882 ; Basil 3 Oct 1829; Toler b 15th Feb 1834 (lost at sea); Gray, Robert James b 18 Feb 1841

Blanche Eliza 1826 - Aug 1911; Anna Frances 13 Sept 1827 - 5 July 1873 = Alfred Darby; James Vincent 15 Nov 1828 - 15 Nov 1838; Mary Eliza 29 Jan 1831 - 5th Dec 1853; Elizabeth b 14th Feb 1832 = William Alexander Jennings; William Legge b 2rd or 5th Nov 1833; Ellen Gray 1 Feb 1839 - 18th March 1839; Richard

At Roscomroe – Ireland

Figure 5 Roscomroe Medieval Church - Richard Chuck 2017

The year was 1826. High up in the fork of an old apple tree in Roscomroe orchard, was seated Miss Margaret Grey, aged fourteen. As it was holiday time, she was relaxing and had left in her Paris finishing school all the rules of correct deportment, and all the instruction she had been given on the simple and elegant courtesies of social life!

She hung up her Leghorn hat by its green ribbons, and surveyed the landscape. It was possible to see anyone coming down the road, and she was

> The contents of Uncle Basil's family diary are still in existence. The current copy was prepared around the be- ginning of WWI from an unpublished manuscript by Basil Gray b. 1768. The later period was added by his grand- daughter, Eliza May (nee Anderson) and Kate Dougharty. An identical note book is owned by Charles Brandram Jones in England which traces the French Gray line of the family. Extracts from this are referred to as Family Note Book (FNB) A summary of the Gray Family Tree may be found in Appendix B

looking out for her father and brother, Humphrey, senior and junior, to return from the barracks. It was early yet and as there was no sign of them, she gazed instead at dear old Roscomroe, the home of her family for generations.

Built solidly, two storeys of blue stone, it had cream-pointed, round-topped mullioned windows, and on the roof, were two pepper-pot topped powder rooms. The chimney-stacks too, were a curious and interesting shape. The wings at each end of the house made it almost crescent-shaped,

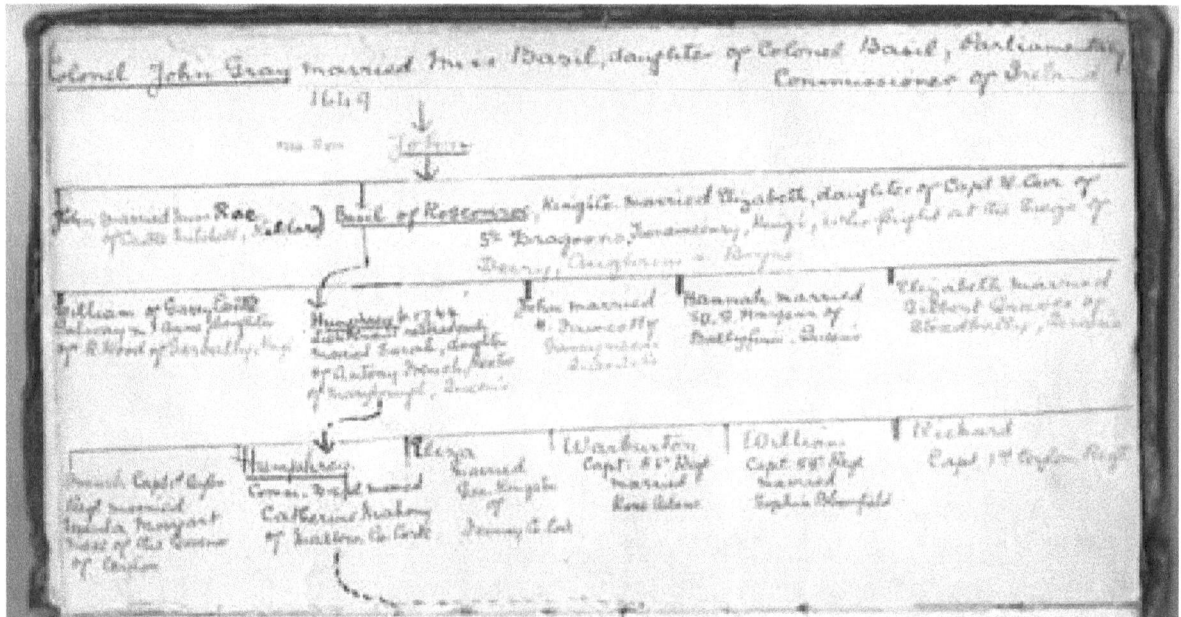

Figure 6 Family Tree from Family Note Book (FNB)

and gave the impression that it held out welcoming arms to any relations and friends who came to visit the family. There was always room for them. Today, the old house looked happily asleep. Only Mrs. Grey and Uncle Quain waited on the terrace where they would have tea. There was not the usual coming and going of Redcoats. The Greys had always been soldiers. Only the day be- fore, Uncle Basil had shown Margaret the Family Diary, begun in 1649 and continued by him in 1826.

Colonel John Grey had come from Scotland to Ireland in 1649 and had married the daughter of Colonel Basil. Their grandson, Basil, had married Elizabeth, daughter of Colonel Carr of the 5th Dragoons, and had fought at Boyne and Aughrim and Basil had built and lived in Roscomroe.

His two sons were William and Humphrey. The elder owned Garry Castle, Galway. Humphrey, born in 1744, continued at Roscomroe. He became Margaret's grandfather. He was in the army for a short time, but

> **Lt Colonel John Gray** was in- deed part of Oliver Cromwell's foray into Ireland in 1649. Oliver was man small in stature with a bloated ego and a penchant for genocide. He was also broke which came from years of war, killing a king and being hit with a severe economic depression. As a result he had no money to pay his troops but not one to be de- terred he simply offered them land in exchange for wages. The fact that others, mainly Catholic, already owned the land was just a mere inconvenience and nothing that a little ethnic cleansing. Read more in Volume Two

retired early. His five sons were all soldiers, so it was no wonder that Margaret's brother, Humphrey, now aged seventeen, thought of none but an army career. The family Christian names occurred often — Basil, Humphrey, Warburton, French - each was the name of Grey bride who perpetuated it by giving it to her son.

The only deviation from entering the Army was when Dennis became a midshipman in the Royal Navy in 1798, but he died of black fever in the West Indies.

His uniform, with its gold, concave buttons, his dirk, untarnished bythe years was under the portrait of a bright-faced boy in the hall at Roscomroe. Even the one Grey who had taken Holy Orders was an Army chaplain in Kotree, India.

In Margaret's youth, it was quite usual to hear father, uncles and cousins spoken of as Major William, Colonel Humphrey, Major Basil, with no surname at all. She suddenly had an absurd idea. Wouldn't it be fun and wouldn't it light up the old place if out of each window or chimney, there popped the powdered or un-powdered head (according to date) and red-coat of all the men who had lived there?

Spoils of War
Lt Colonel John Gray was a recipient of Crom- wellian favours for land and received his at Ballycurragh, a townland adjoining Aghancon and The Leap. When he arrived Gray was likely to have been met with the icy silence of despair and devastation for miles around. Ironically, this was largely due to the actions of his army compatriots when, 'in the spring of 1650, General John Reynolds marched from Kilkenny with twelve thousand men to subdue Laois and Offaly. He destroyed eve- rything in his path – castles, monasteries and churches. When his army had passed through, there was nothing left only desola- tion. Gray's life was very different now with other challenges of caring for his young wife, Mary Basil and their son John and daughters. Read more in Volume Two.

When the present ones approached, wouldn't they get a shock to see them all marching-out and lining up on the terrace? Except for three, none had risen above the rank of Major. They had not really been very fortunate. Death or permanent injuries had spoiled or prematurely ended their careers. If Margaret had been able to read the future, she would have seen, in 1838, handsome Lieutenant Basil Grey, lamed and ruined through his defense of Newport, receiving from Queen Victoria his Majority promotion and the thanks of Parliament for conspicuous bravery. Then almost a century later, Denis Grey, aged seventeen, mentioned in dispatches after Gallipoli, and Richard Jones, his cousin, aged nineteen, making a valiant effort leading eight men to delay the German rush on Vimy Ridge in 1915, posthumously awarded the Victoria Cross. Her sisters' descendants too, would give all they had, not counting the cost, in determination to keep their country free. All could claim kinship through Roscomroe.

Lt Basil Grey – Newport

Lieutenant Basil Grey was in charge of the defence of the Westgate Hotel in Newport from the Chartists a working class movement supporting Parliamentary Reform in Britain. The Chartist riot in Newport on 4th November 1839 resulted in over 20 deaths, as well as many wounded and arrested. Ironically, several of those arrested were sent to VDL. It would appear that Basil was badly wounded. More information is available on the Chartist Ances- tors web page and Frost, J. (1986) *The Trial of John Frost for High Treason* (Vol. 2).

Denis Gray, son of Basil and Louise Warburton and b1896 was on Active Service with the 2nd Expeditionary Force from Australia in the Great War of the Allies against Germany. In 1915 he was at Gallipoli, where he was wounded, in France was wounded again and later buried for hours but dug out alive though unconscious. Was mentioned in dispatches 1918 because with 2 men, he killed 8 German machine gunners and captured 10 Germans.' (FNB)

While Miss Margaret Grey sat and dreamed, time was passing. It was after five and she suddenly realised that the Humphreys were late. She decided to jump down and be ready to meet them, when they would come, laughing and brown, from the parade ground. She had just seen a flash of scarlet; so she smoothed her red-gold curls that the breeze had ruffled, and put on her Leghorn. Papa liked her to be careful of her rose and cream skin!

Richard Jones

Richard Basil Brandram Jones did not return. VC 'Richard in 1915 at the age of 17, went into active service in France as 1st Lieut of the Loyal North Lancashire, after a year's training at Aldershot. He was killed in action on 21st May 1916. His Regt the L.N.L had been in most terrible fighting for some days & was greatly praised for (great) gal- lantry. They captured & held a crater at Vimy in France against great odds. Dick was called up on Saturday night at 11p.m. to keep guard & on Sunday, a terrific bombardment commenced. He stood in the front of the parapet on the Ridge at Vimy with his men & coolly shot 15 Germans. He was wounded in the head & with great bravery, rose and fired again, was shot in the head again & died saying "I'm done" – His mother received a splendid letter from a fellow officer in which he said "Hero in life as death – he was always ready & cheerful to do his duty." (FNB) The King presented his father with the Victoria Cross and is now held at his school, Dulwich College London who sent the im- ages with kind permission of the Governors of Dulwich College.
Richard is still remembered by his family in England a century later. A commemoration was held on the centenary of Richard's death in Lon- don with full military honours.

1 Humphrey Grey's Silver Pocket Watch cira 1829 made by
Richard Widenham and case by William Rowland

Then she began to run, but after a few steps stood still. They had not seen her and she noticed that her father was not as erect as usual. He seemed to be leaning on young Humphrey and both looked serious and troubled. They had stopped and without speaking, were gazing at dear, lovely Roscomroe. Why? What did it mean? Surely not war again! Margaret remembered that her father had fought at Londonderry, but that was long ago. Her soft cheeks lost their roses and her blue-grey eyes, veiled by long black-tipped lashes, suddenly became very anxious, but she smiled gaily and called "Humphreys!" She was so small and dainty in her lilac muslin that their faces lightened as each held out a hand to her.

"Oh," she called, "you are naughty! Mamma, Uncle Quain and I are just dying of starvation. You are late!"

She thought young Humphrey's lip quivered but her father smiling at her said: "We must make our apologies. We are sorry to have kept you and Mamma waiting but Margaret, we met Cousin William (Major William Gray) and you know what that means!" Margaret did know — she asked no more questions. She had

Roscomroe Mansion Roscomroe is in King's County, now Offaly. The name had some resonance in the family folklore. It had been the primary seat of the   Gray family   since
John Gray's grandson, Basil moved therein the late 1730s. It was sold in 1808. It is likely that Humphrey was born there and spent his formative years grow- ing up in the area.
Read more in Volume Two

more than once been Cousin William's audience, and had failed to get a word in edgeways. Much as she liked him this could be very trying. Cousin William and Cousin James (Lt James Gray) her father's first cousins, once removed, lived a few miles away at Garry Castle. The former, a Major of the 94th had gone to Africa with Mungo Park and had helped to discover the source of the Niger. For his services there, the Government had offered him a grant of land in any British colony, and now he was seriously considering accepting it. He

Major Gray Expedition

Major William Gray 94th Regt married 1822 Ellen (Eleanor Toler) daughter of William Kingsley of Rockford Nenagh Co. Tippererary. For his services in exploring the Source of the Niger (Africa) he received from Government a grant of land in (VDL). Died at Rockford, Avoca, Tasmania.' The irony is that he never actually set eyes on the on the River Niger, it is more of a family myth than reality

had a charming wife Ellen and very young sons. Being in the Army for generations was not very lucrative, and with continual wars and resulting disabilities, he was beginning to doubt whether he could give his children the way of living and the education that his forefathers had given him.

William wondered if it would not be better to make a clean break and begin life afresh in a new land. It would mean farming and he knew nothing of that, but he could get a good, experienced man to go with him.

He had heard that farming could be a comfortable life. Besides he would not go alone. His brother James married to Mary Legge, said he would take up land to which he also was entitled, and would try his fate with him. They had not fully decided, but had had good reports of Van Diemen's Land, and liked the sound of it so much, that they were already making up their minds to resign send in their papers and go there.

> Why Emigrate? Each family had their own rea- sons for leaving Ireland depending on personality, personal circumstances and the economic challenges of that period in Ireland.
> Read more VOLUME TWO BOX FOUR: REASONS TO EMIGRATE

Though Margaret did not know it they were most anxious to get her father to join them. They agreed that he had a better business head and more common sense than any of them and they felt it would be a great asset to have him too. If a small colony of Greys went overseas, they would not feel so lost! No wonder Humphrey Senior was feeling worried! If they went it meant that Humphrey Junior, his only son, must sacrifice his hope of following family tradition but the boy, always unselfish and considerate, must be allowed to decide for himself.

Then his mother, Catherine, and four little sisters must be provided for. Uncle Quain (on the maternal side) was a clever barrister and had always had the family affairs in hand. He had been warning them lately that Irish stocks, from which most of their income was derived, were low on the market and

> Uncle Quain is mentioned several times and for those who like detail this is their relationship to the Greys. 'Margaret, sister of Kate Mahony (Humphrey Grey's wife) married John Quain and had 3 sons: Richard, baronet and Queen's Physician, (who had a first cousin also Sir Richard Quain) Sir John QC Judge of Ireland Dr Jones Quain who died at age 25. Sir R Quain married Lady Middlton, Vicountess. The brother of Margaret and Kate Mahony was John Mahony, Recorder of Titles, Dublin' (FNB)

that owing to the potato blight some of their tenant farmers were unable to pay their rents and were not taking fresh leases, but were emigrating instead.

The family would soon feel the depression, Uncle Quain said. He himself, had been feeling it for some time and was particularly concerned for his young sons, fearing he might not be able to send them to the University. There were no scholarships, but Humphrey and his wife, proud of their young nephews, had been able to advance their fees, and they had already begun their brilliant careers.

Richard, the elder, later received a baronetcy, and was to become one of Queen Victoria's surgeons and write "Quain's Anatomy" studied by all medical students of the day. John, some years younger, was later to write to his relations in Van Diemen's Land, to say that he was a Judge of the High Court. But this was all in the far future and Margaret trotting between the Humphreys to keep up with their long strides, got them quickly to the tea table where Mamma and Uncle Quain with the rest of the family waited. They were Catherine aged thirteen, Henrietta and little

> The preparation for young women to go to the far-flung corners of the British Empire was to go to finishing school in Paris and learn all the ne- cessities of becoming a gentlewoman. The primary text for their education was written by Richmal Mangnall (1769– 1820) and became a mainstay for teachers during most of the 19th Century. Its full title is: Mangnall, R. (1859). Historical and miscel- laneous questions for the use of young people. Longman, Brown, Green, Longmans & Roberts.

dancing Lysbeth (Sarah Elizabeth). They all had something to tell "Papa," who loved this hour and everyone encouraged them to chatter. Tea-time was fun time!

Afterwards Biddy their young nurse took all three for a walk, then bath and bed while Margaret and her mother watered the garden. The two Humphreys settled down to an anxious worried talk with Quain. He had nothing cheerful to tell them. Things were very bad indeed. He was reluctant to advise them in any way. He knew their love for Roscomroe, and could realise the wrench it would be to leave it and their ordered way of living. He doubted if Mrs. Gray, William and James' mother, though she would make no complaint, would be able to stand the rigours of colonial life. She was always frail, and had led a sheltered life.

The Decision

After many consultations Humphrey, William and James came to a decision. They would not throw the burden of deciding on to their wives. That was their responsibility. The conclusion was that William and James would go ahead to Van Diemen's Land with their families and while Humphrey kept an eye on things at home. If these showed no signs of improvement and the cousins sent satisfactory reports of their new life then Humphrey, his family and the three servants who wished to accompany them would arrange with others wishing to emigrate and charter a sailing vessel and fol- low. They were all entitled to land grants and would take out sufficient capital to add to their acreage and would take as much stock as possible with them.

Meanwhile Margaret and Catherine, ignorant of impending changes in their lives, were packed off for another year at the finishing school in Paris. Their parents were afraid that they might find it difficult to find facilities for education "down under," so no time must be wasted. In Paris they would study all that a gentlewoman should know — the use of the globe, embroidering, the piano-forte, so that on social occasions they might contribute a few songs or melodies, how to make pretty little paintings, mostly flower studies, to converse easily in French, which was much used in social circles, and to understand a smattering of Italian. To recognise operas and to write charming little letters without blot or erasure.

For general knowledge they had to learn by heart the answers to Magnall's Questions (like a modern quiz). What is coal? and so on. Spelling was taught in an easy way for the teacher! Margaret had to learn ten words for her first preparation. The next day she waited, pencil in hand, expecting to be dictated to but not a bit of it! The Frenchwoman repeated, *"Ecrivez vos mots, mademoiselle*," and when Margaret looked at her in a puzzled way she explained that in her school, pupils had to learn words straight down the column and write all from memory!

The girls also learnt all the current dances including the graceful minuet and by diligent use of the backboard and moving with a block on their heads they acquired a lightness and quickness in walking which was delightful to see. They also practiced the graceful and correct manner of entering a room or carriage, and gained an ease of manner and charm of deportment which lasted and distinguished them through life. When they returned to Roscomroe their parents were delighted with their progress. Each had a gentle, pretty poise, especially Catherine who carried her head delightfully. The girls were equally charmed to be at home until the sad news of the projected

> Individual Reasons for Leaving
> It is easier to understand James' and William's reason for leaving on such an adventure than it is for their older cousin (once removed) Humphrey1. Both were considerably younger and had served in the army, possibly in the latter part of the Napoleonic War. As part payment for ser- vice, soldiers, were offered land in VDL. Their great grandfather, Lt Colonel John Gray, had also been granted land in Ireland for his army ser- vice. How history repeats itself!
> Read more in Volume Two.

move ruined their happiness. Young though they were they had sufficient self-control to make no outcry. Their father explained the necessity for the move and they had no need to be told what a sorrow it was for him nor how disappointing for Humphrey. They had been taught at home and abroad that a true gentle-woman puts consideration for others before herself but at night, in the room they shared, they wept bitterly.

Every day there were sad farewells. It was an extra grief to them all that they could not take horses. Only bullocks were used for transport in Van Diemen's Land. Even the girls had been able to ride since they were four years old, and Humphrey and his father were in the habit of attending the country meets, and now this pleasure must be renounced. However, they sold the horses to buyers who promised to sell them back if the opportunity of sending them to Van Diemen's Land arose.

Meanwhile, preparations went well. Various friends, wishing to travel with them, had combined to charter a vessel, and they had chosen one named *Letitia*. The captain had good references and would engage a crew. They had been invited to farewell parties so Major and Mrs. Grey felt they must have a dinner party for his fellow officers. They had it and owing to one unusual feature it was long remembered, for on the side table, whole, was the most magnificent salmon ever seen in the district. It had been sent to Mrs. Grey by a great angler. She thanked him graciously but inwardly quaked. How in the world could they cook it without break- ing it? Certainly no fish-kettle could hold it! But Mattie, the cook, a widow who had been with them for years, felt her skill challenged and she did not intend to let Roscomroe down.

After pondering deeply, she said to Mrs. Grey, "Why, sure, Mam, we can do it. Use the washing copper! No one will know." Mrs. Grey was startled, but she knew Mattie to be scrupulously clean, so agreed, and when she heard all the admiration the sight of the fish aroused, she said innocently, "Isn't it wonderful? But I have a cook who can do any- thing!" Afterwards she told Mattie all the compliments she received and they had a good laugh. Mattie was a tower of strength! She and her son, Paddy Barnes, were prepared to go to the end of the earth with the Greys, so they took it for granted that they would go to V.D.L. too. Mattie was given two cases, one for her personal belongings and the other for kitchen requirements. Some of her clothes got short shrift when she stuffed in amongst them, a big iron kettle and some heavy iron sauce- pans. Indeed when she went on board, underneath her inherited green Donegal cape her two favourite pots were tied securely round her waist. She had every intention of interviewing and routing the cook in his galley, making him clearly understand that if she wished to cook there she would brook no interference. She was however so smiling and confident that he soon wondered if the galley were his or hers!

The Departure

There was so much to think over. The girls wrote long lists for their mother of china, cutlery, glass, linen and a little of their old furniture. A big couch, some Chippendale chairs and the harpsichord on which they had already learnt their notes. Some books and rugs, a few home remedies for colds, beds, but not the beautiful four- poster which they hoped to get out later on, also wearing apparel for all seasons (were there any shops in V.D.L.?). They packed very few ornaments and only one or two pictures and lastly a painting by an artistic Grey of their home Roscomroe. Everything must be ready a week before sailing. The two Humphreys packed the best available farm implements. They also bought clothes and hats suit- able for the climate. Letters from V.D.L. made suggestions about what to bring and hopefully they packed good riding outfits.

The question of food was very pressing. In 1826, no fruits or vegetables could be preserved for long, so when those they had were used, then they must trust to getting more at various ports. Captain Cook's early experience taught them to get cases of lemons or limes to prevent scurvy, to which those who were obliged to live on salted butter and meat were susceptible. No tins of powdered or preserved milk had yet appeared, so Betsy, the little cow, had to travel with them, in the anxious care of Paddy Barnes. They hoped, if possible, to get a goat, for the Greys were not the only children on board, and milk was precious. There were a few crates of fowls and eggs, as a special treat. No one thought of preserving any. Lastly, a sow and piglets.

The last two or three days at Roscomroe were crowded. Neighbours came to bid them farewell, bringing gifts that they hoped would be useful. Young men feeling the stir of adventure called to note all the preparations. Many of them were Humphrey's fellow officers, eager to hear all they could. They sent messages or letters to friends in New South Wales or Van Diemen's Land with rather sketchy addresses. Ideas of geography were vague in those days and there was no post. A letter might be addressed —

Mrs. Prim,
New South Wales,
New Zealand and Van Diemen's Land.
So it was just a matter of luck where it did land!

The Greys were asked to take delivery of a number of letters and, guessing what a joy it must be to receive them, undertook to do their best, but it was understood that it might be a year or more before the right owner was found. On board, Mrs. Grey tried not to sigh when she saw the cramped saloon, narrow cabins and hard berths, which were to comprise their home for many months. The two elder girls understood, and with Mattie's help, tried to make things as comfortable as possible. Elizabeth and Henrietta did not worry. Everything to them was exciting and it was only because of Biddy's anxious care that they did not go head foremost down the hold. They were determined to miss nothing.

> Their journey as we know was not un- eventful mainly as a result of the shipwreck of the *Letitia* which is now well documented by Frank Murray. He has created a website called *My Early Pioneers and Their Lives* which follows the families and individuals who survived the experience at St Jago, most of whom continued to Australia.

The sea was not very friendly for a few days and no one was very happy. Then the gentlemen on board made a startling discovery. They knew very little about sailing but apparently the crew, who had come aboard simply as means of getting to the colony, knew even less and in spite of his forcible language the Captain gave them little inducement to learn. He seemed to know his job and fortunately as it turned out the younger men took every chance to learn about the rigging and steering and would climb up the masts daily watching the coastline and looking out for passing craft. The Captain had not been long at sea when he appeared to have a mighty thirst and was often incapable so the passengers had not only to put their new Knowledge to the test but also had to take over the management of the crew.

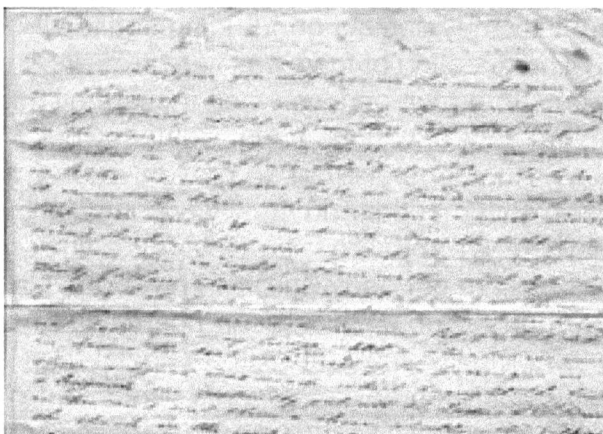

2 Copy of part of the original letter describing the shipwreck

The voyage was a tremendous trial of endurance for the mothers. The food and accommodation question, the anxiety about the health of their families and their own health.

There were no doctors aboard and the constant not-to-be-spoken-of worry as to what lay at the end of the journey was always with them. Yet there were days they enjoyed. The ship looking beautiful sailed on a calm sea with an even keel and they sat on deck in the sunshine. There were dreadful days too when the little ship was only a cockle-shell tossed on mountainous waves. All women and children were battened down below and not allowed on deck. Their menkind, weary and worn did not dare go to bed except for short intervals.

Then Mattie, a good sailor, rose to the occasion. She took supreme. command of the galley and was able to produce hot stews and boiling drinks at all hours. Like Charles Dicken's Mrs. Gummidge, so many men wanted to marry her, that she threatened to empty a bucket of dirty water over them if they persisted!

They must have been at sea a month when Humphrey wrote to his cousin.

Dear John,

I suppose you will hear ere this reaches you of our shipwreck. We are thank God all safe with an entire loss of property except for a few torn rags that we got on the shore, next day. On the 15th August we came to anchor at Porto Prayo Island off St. Jago to take in water as what we had on board was very bad. It came on to blow, which occasioned a swell and the ship rolled much. It was deemed advisable to let go the second anchor, which was neglected by the Captain.

We were then in eight fathoms water with less than thirty fathoms chain out, and about 3 o'clock on the evening of the 19th she parted her anchor, the chain breaking then too late the second anchor was let go, but did not hold. You may judge what a situation we were in leaving the boat and getting most of the passengers on shore a signal was made which brought the boat alongside. We instantly got all the Ladies and Children in her and sent them ashore. Shortly after 4 o'clock, she struck on the rocks, in a dreadful surf.

She soon began to fill and her masts to roll which made it dangerous to stay near her. I remained on board till her lower deck was forced up to the upper one. I am sorry to say that no exertion was made to save the ship or cargo. The wind abated before the anchor broke. I wanted Clements to let the kedge anchor be run from the ship, but he would take no notice of what anyone said.

We can never give thanks sufficient to the Almighty. Had it happened by night I think five would not be saved. From the great heat of the weather the Ladies had only a gown and the Gentlemen a jacket and trousers and in that state we are now obliged to remain for want of others to change them. I have seen some shipwrecks but any thing to equal this I never witnessed. She was actually torn in pieces. We have experienced much kindness from Mr. Goodwin, the British Consul, who provided us with provisions and lodgings during our stay and a passage for as many as wished to go to Rio de Janeiro.

We left some of our passengers on the Island of St. Jago, who intend returning to Ireland by America, viz, Mr. Page, son to Mr Page, stockbroker Dublin, Mr. Bell [Hill], Dublin, Mr. Roberts, near Derry and Dr. Clerk, of Shiliness [Skibbereen], Mrs. Weston and child of Cork went on in the Mary of London next day. She did not save a stitch of clothing nor a shilling of money Mr. Murphy, of Dublin, also went in the Mary.

We have on board the Hesperus of New York, Captain Allen Master bound to Rio, Mr. Moore of Dublin wife four children and servants, Mr. Pentland (the sea fur cargo) [supercargo] Mr Org [Onge] Dublin. Captain Moriarty wife child and two friends of his steerage passengers, Captain G[C]lement's wife and two children Mr. L. W. Clerk Shiliness [Skibbereen], Mr. Popham from near Bandon also part of our former crew.

I must give you an account of our proceedings since we left Cork Harbour. We were sent to sea with the worst crew that were ever shipped on board any vessel. They could hardly work her out of Cove repeatedly the Pilot said the crew knew nothing about the management of the ship. Mr. Harris the Customs House Officer, where he was taking leave of Captain Moriarty's child said, "My dear I wish you may arrive in New South Wales but I foresee it will not be in the Letitia!"

We had only five hands on board that knew anything about seamanship, and three of them were as great villains as could be met with. They were picked up in Cove as the crew that shipped on board in Dublin left her in Cove. Repeatedly these fellows said the ship would be lost for want of hands to work her. Clements said he would put into Madeira and ship three or four [more] hands. Instead of doing so he went into the harbour and on finding the Port charges would be about six pounds he stood out to sea putting us at the mercy of the waves, with a promise to put into Pernambuco for water and fresh provisions. Our water was bad four days after we left Cork as the casks that contained it was bad and dirty.

Almost every day we had a row between Captain, Mate and crew. We were blessed with a fair wind from two days after we sailed, until we anchored in Porta Prayo.

Arrived in Rio de Janeiro on Sunday, Oct. 5th after a passage of 39 days from St. Jago, and came to lodge at Hotel de Lempire on Oct., 8th., 1828.

IN RIO DE JANEIRO

There they lived for about five months in spite of many anxious enquiries in search of a suitable ship in which to continue their journey. At first it had been delightful to be on solid ground— have comfortable beds and good, though strangely prepared, food, but the terrible experiences they had been through and the knowledge that they had not reached their journey's end, made them long to leave. Also they had lost all their possessions so carefully selected and packed with which they had intended to furnish their new home.

Not one of the party could understand or speak Portuguese, and though there was a British Consul they could turn to, they longed to be with their own people. Fortunately, at the time of the wreck, Major Humphrey had been wearing a belt of sovereigns, which he had brought for contingencies, and he got these ashore safely, so there was enough for immediate necessities and the Consul was very ready to help. The children found everything exciting — they were too young to worry. With Martha and Biddy, they explored the very narrow streets of the town with their over- hanging balconies from which they could hear the voices and the lutes of lovers. They could not go out in the heat of the day. It was usually at dusk just before their bedtime that they went until Mrs. Grey realised that they were picking up the language and its meaning, much too quickly for her peace of mind yet she could not keep them indoors all day.

The streets in Rio were curious in some respects. There was no mixture of different types of shops. The whole of one street might be shoe shops, the next all riding necessities and so on. Mrs. Grey veiled herself and the girls like the Portuguese women, for Margaret's golden-haired beauty and the fresh-ness of their complexions had been attracting rather embarrassing attentions.

Soon after landing, the Governor of the district who had heard of the ship-wreck sent to make kind enquiries and to invite the men of the party with the Consul to dinner at Government House. Everything was beautiful, but it was entirely a man's dinner, neither a sign nor mention of ladies so they took it for granted the Governor was unmarried. He sent beautiful flowers and fruit to the Hotel for the ladies and shortly afterwards called on them. He was a clever good-looking man with charming manners and liked to send his carriage and invite the whole family to take historical excursions with him, when he was out on circuit.

He was particularly charming to Margaret so her parents were not altogether surprised when at the end of a year he asked her hand in marriage. She really liked him.

They all did but her father would not let her be pressed for an answer. She was after all not quite seventeen and the Governor twice her age. Would she be happy with a foreigner and speaking a different language though that trouble would soon be got over. But the life would be so strange to any she had known and she would have to change her religion to his.

"No", her father decided. He thanked the Governor for the honour he wished to pay them, said he would tell Margaret but added that no pressure must be brought on her. He thought it might be six months or more before she would be expected to decide. She was very astonished when told. Though she knew that all girls married at seventeen or eighteen, she did not want to live far from her own people.

At last a suitable ship was found and passages for all were taken on her. Mrs. Grey had bought what china and furniture she could to replace what had been lost as nearly as possible. This as well as a large quantity of tobacco bought by the Humphrey and his friends had been sent on board. The cousins though neither he nor they cared for smoking had written saying it was much sought after in V.D.L. and as it grew profusely in Rio it might be a good speculation to bring some with them. The Greys had also been able to get a few fowls and another Betsy, though she was a reminder of the poor little one they had heard mooing at sea.

It was only a week before leaving. The Governor had gone off on circuit, but had written to say he would return two days before they left. He hoped that Margaret would think over and then accept his proposal. They need take no trouble about the wedding. He would see to everything. Her parents talked over things anxiously. If Margaret married him she would be certain of care and luxury and the life in V.D.L. was so uncertain.

The day before they expected the Governor the Greys all went for a country drive to a part they had not seen before. Practically all their luggage was on board so they had nothing to worry about. As they drove along they admired the very beautiful harbour and then noticed a fine white house in a lovely terraced garden. The Humphrey said to the driver of their coach "Whose house is that?" and the man smiling replied, "That senhor is the house for the Governor's ladies." Humphrey could not believe his ears. He looked, with horror at Humphrey his son who was listening then said "Do you mean His Excellency's mother and sisters?" "Oh no," said the man still smiling, "I mean the wives of Don Ameche. Perhaps the senhor does not know he has three?"

The Senhor did not! He lost his breath for a moment. He let the drive go on as planned then told the man they must return to the Hotel and on the way was quietly and quickly telling Humphrey what he had planned. He knew it would only lead to trouble to confront the villain and tell him exactly what he thought of him.

They must smuggle their dear beautiful Margaret on board and keep her hidden until they had sailed. They would drive near the ship *Ann* and then Humphrey, the girls and Biddy, would ask to be allowed to walk and go to the ship. This was not unusual as they had been there several times. The parents would say that they wished to go to the Hotel and rest but their brother Humphrey would accompany the girls to their cabin. He would promise to explain later to Margaret then go off to consult the Captain, a fine trustworthy man. Should the Captain have finished loading he might, considering the circumstances and that the Greys were the largest party on board, arrange to get out to sea by an earlier tide. The Greys would notify the other passengers and they would all be safely away before Ameche returned to cause trouble.

The parents, Martha and Barnes would take their usual evening walk but this time would go on board and as soon as possible the captain would put off to sea. His father told Humphrey to lock the girls in their cabin and stay near it. He felt so furious poor man and so insulted. Should he write and put in plain words what he thought of Ameche? No, the only thing to do was to run away. Everything turned out as they had planned. Martha with her son Barnes quickly grasped the situation. She took his arm and in her cloak and mantilla with a new pot under each arm went on board. But she was determined before she left to get even with the Don.

She was not surprised to hear of his villainy! She had never liked him in spite of his good looks and charm. Never, never, would he have been good enough for her lovely Miss Margaret. She knew of the costly gifts he had tried to bring Margaret and that only flowers and fruit had been accepted. But several times lately beautiful glass vases had accompanied the flowers and it seemed paltry to return these so Martha, taking a last look into Margaret's room and telling no one, threw the flowers on the floor and trampled on them. Then with her shoe she smashed the vases and added the pieces to the flowers.

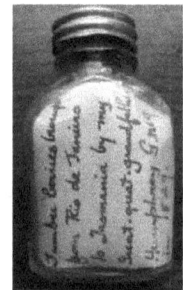

That was the only message left for Don Ameche. He came bearing exquisite flowers and was told the birds had flown. He couldn't believe it and insisted on seeing Margaret's room hoping for a note but all he saw was Martha's work because the usual Portuguese "manaňa" (to-morrow) the room not being in use had been left untouched. Humiliation indeed for a proud man and by the time his first rage had expended itself on everyone near he had to realise that British subjects on a British ship on the high seas were untouchable.

3 Juniper berries bought by family

OFF AGAIN

Poor Mrs. Grey! In her wildest dreams she could not have imagined that it would be heaven to lie on a hard berth in a narrow ships cabin, but oh, the relief of knowing that once more they were amongst their own countrymen and that no unforeseen danger threatened them! Every morning after breakfast they would have morning prayers and give thanks for the day's safe journey and in her thoughts, she would add "I thank Thee O God that Margaret is still with us." It seemed she could not bear any of her family out of her sight and the ship being small made things easy for her.

It could not be said that Margaret in spite of the terror from which she had escaped refrained from mischief and from causing havoc amongst eligible males. She had only to lift her long lashes and look at them admiringly when they climbed down from the rigging, up which they went daily for them to land at her feet. Humphrey junior took her to task more than once but after a short time gave it up. The minx could look so troubled and so innocent! Let them look after them- selves!

Catherine was more reserved and shy so was little Henrietta with her very big deep blue eyes, her aquiline nose and long silky brown plaits. She was such a wise little woman, loving to mother, her dolls or anyone who was kind enough to have a headache! She had one great friend on board, John Thompson a young Scot, the son of a ship owner who was on his way to see what trade could be done between V.D.L. and India by their ships. He was so gentle and kind even made a house for the dolls and he had been about the world with his father. Mrs. Grey was pleased when he came to show them the wonders of the sea, a school of porpoises playing happily near the ship or flying fish, like fluorescent birds in the light of shining waves, Henrietta was the baby of the ship and her mother, Biddy and the girls were always on the watch countering the effect of the young lady's getting too much attention. She was such a gay happy little person.

On one occasion Biddy who had been in charge was horrified to discover Lysbeth climbing up the rigging to the applause of an irresponsible youth above her. Biddy was too frightened to call her but quickly got a sailor who rescued her then dragged the youth down and gave him such a trouncing that he dared not go near the masts for days. Biddy took the pink- cheeked culprit to her mother who decreed that she must do nothing without telling the others and the two elder girls would give her and Lysbeth two hours tuition daily in reading, writing and sewing. Henrietta did not shine in the last, but what can you expect from one so young? Henrietta would contentedly sew long seams or make clothes for her dolls. She learned quickly and by the end of the voyage she could read as well as any of them and even recite short poems. She was always devoted to Catherine, who taught her.

> The following are the passengers per brig Anne, Captain Samuel Cornby, which arrived at this port, on the 3d instant, from Rio Janeiro, Captain and Mrs. Moriarty and three children, Mr. Mrs. and Miss

The arrival and news of the fate of the Letitia was well known in the Colony with considerable support and welcoming of the new settlers. The Hobart-Town Courier shared the story and o its readers on the 12th June 1829;

the passengers per brig Anne, Captain Samuel Cornby, which arrived at this port, on the 3d instant, from Rio Janeiro, Captain and Mrs. Moriarty and three children, Mr. Mrs. and Miss Moore, and 3 children, Mr. Gray, Mr. Foster, Mr.Macnamara, Mr. Riley, Mr. and Mrs. Mc Ghie, and three children, Mrs. Clarke and Mrs. Huggard, all originally passengers per Letitia, from London, Captain Clements, late of the Colonial vessel Glory. Passengers from Rio- Mr. Malony, also John Ring Matthew Mayes, Darby Cleary, John Cashman, Dan Heily, Patrick Murray, and John Leaky ; Labourers from Ireland who emigrated to Rio and being in distress, were forwarded by the British Consul, to this port. The Letitia was wrecked on the 19th August, last, at St Jago, with 60 persons on board. They re- mained at St. Jago 8 days, the British Consul then hired an American vessel to take them to Rio, at which place they remained (with the exception of 11) 5 months, and the British Consul humanely paid for their lodging and diet, and chartered the Ann for this place for £900. The 11 of the passen- gers and crew, which remained at St Jago, (by their own desire) all died of fever, and were buried in one spot. A fever broke out among the passengers between St. Jago and Rio, and 7 died.The passengers per Letitia, lost all their properly, among which was £11,00 in specie, belonging to Mr. Gray, who has arrived with his family at this port. The cargo of the Ann is consigned to order, with the exception of 668 baskets of tobacco, for Mr. Gray, a passenger.
THE HOBART-TOWN COURIER. (189, June 13). The Hobart Town Courier (Tas. : 1827 - 1839), p. 2. A day later the Colonial Times on the 12th June 1829 highlighted its support for the families and urged the Governor to look favourably on their predicament

The rest of the voyage passed without any unusual incident. There were calm days or storm, the passengers taking everything philosophically in hope of the Utopia which they expected ahead. They spent a week in South Africa pro- visioning and there went for drives, seeing all they could. One man owner of a big property, met them at a friend's home and invited them all to his beautiful Dutch House. He was unmarried and, like Don Ameche, found Margaret's beauty devastating and begged her father to consider him as a son-in- law. Made wary by the Rio experience Humphrey refused to promise more than that the suitor (who had offered to make a settlement on her of £40,000 equal to £100,000 later) should hear from him from V.D.L. after Margaret's wishes were ascertained. According to promise, he answered later "Margaret does not think she could live so far from us all and we will not bring any pressure to bear on her. Her happiness is very dear to us all. Thank you, but our answer is No." The suitor immediately replied that he would be quite ready to sell out and live in any colony she chose. But it was no use. Margaret had no wish to marry.

It was just under one year after leaving Ireland on 20 July 1828 before they arrived in V.D.L. and it was an intense relief to know they had at last reached the promised land. They had an unpleasant passage sailing below the Island but once they entered the Derwent River the beauty of the beauty of the coastline was most comforting.

Figure 10 Grayfort - Richard Chuck

The Arrival

Theirs was not the only ship to arrive on that day the 3rd June 1829. Some carried convicts but even these had an air of hope. Captain James Gray waving frantically gave them a delighted welcome. His bullocks and dray filled with mat- tresses, cushions and rugs waited patiently for them. Other family groups awaited the ship too.

Arriving in Van Diemen's Land
Imagine, if you will, the theatre being played out at Hunter Island Dock in Hobart, Van Die- men's Land on the 20th August 1827. The Ship Medway having anchored is swarmed upon by activity; small boats everywhere, sails, ropes, shouts, men stowing, tying, winching, excitement
Read more in Volume Two

The sun was shining. Every- thing seemed propitious for a restful homecoming. James had engaged rooms at the Cornwall Hotel for the whole party, and there they were to stay until their possessions could be brought ashore and essential china

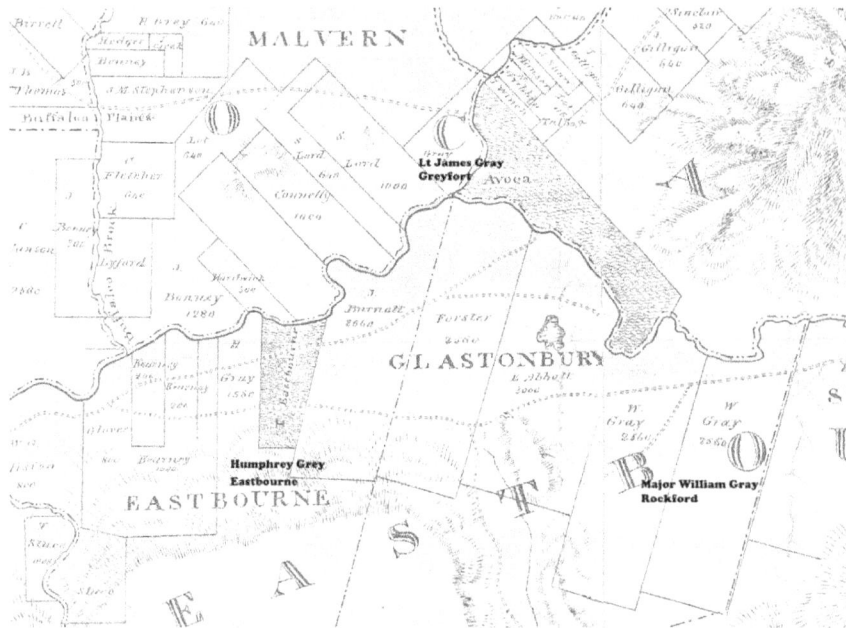

Adapted from Tasmanian Archive and Heritage Office Map of Van Diemen's Land

Houses as a Reflection of Character The decision to emigrate was not only a result of external events but the dis- position of the people involved. Looking at the houses it is easy to see how the character of each man is re- flected in the houses they designed and built. The houses are intriguing. It is rare to have anything left from that time but to be able to relate and match each one to the people who created them is even more fascinating.

Taking into account the nature of the men and times, it is reasonable to as- sume the women had little say such matters. The houses are: Grayfort and Rockford constructed by brothers James and William in the late 1820s. Eastbourne House build by Humphrey in about 1832. Read more in Volume Two

and furniture sent ahead by drays to Avoca to the William Grays, with whom they were to make a home until their own was built. Major William had called his place Rockford, the name of his wife's parents' home in Ireland.

When James built his, he called it Grayfort. Mrs. Grey and party had a much-needed rest. After the cramped ship's quarters the hotel was palatial! Martha and Biddy took the girls for all available walks and though there were no shops and most of the population lived in tents there was quite enough variety to amuse them. Their Mother finding, she might send a few letters to Ireland by the returning ship was writing long crisscrossed ones telling all the perils they had been through; of their safe arrival; and of James' welcome. Sir Rowland Hill had not yet brought in postal reforms so letters travelled through the agency of friends. At that time in England sending one sheet cost four shillings for four hundred miles.

Then there were farewells to their fellow passengers with whom they had become friendly. They might not see one another again for not all had their locations in adjoining districts and unmade roads made transport difficult. Land had then to be cleared, fences and houses built. They could keep in touch only with letters. The Greys' found family news awaiting them. The first letter was from Ceylon from Humphrey's youngest brother Richard (Lieutenant 1st Ceylon Regiment). He wrote the usual long crisscross letter:

My dear Humphrey

I need not describe my astonishment and satisfaction on receipt of a letter from Home, dated 12th of October, addressed to me by Sarah. It arrived on the 14th of March, and therein I find that you and Mrs. Grey are settled in V.D.L., though I regret exceedingly from the tenor of her letter, to hear of the misfortunes that befell you and the remainder of the passengers of your ship, and that you sustained such a considerable loss, but thank God that your lives are spared, together with a thousand sovereigns which Sarah mentioned.

Had I known of your reaching V.D.L. an opportunity offered. of sending you a letter by two officers, viz : Lieut. Fowkes A.D.C. to Sir Edward Barnes, and Lieut. de Lancy, A.D.C. to Sir Hudson Lowe, who expects to be Governor on Sir Edward's departure. They are both particular friends of mine and their interest might have been. of service to you. I understand that N.P. Wright, Judicial Commissioner here, a very worthy man, has a sister married to General Darling, Commandant of N.S.W. Should it be your opinion that a letter having this medium should be of any service to you, I can easily obtain it for you at any time.

Criss-cross letter from Emily Gray 1839

By the Hobart Town papers which Fowkes and de Lancey have brought me, I regret to find that the Aborigines have such a hostile attitude to the settlers. You may rest assured that a mild plan will never answer with individuals of their disposition. They must be given to fear us and there can be no possible way of bringing matters to a close than by using severe means, which is to let them feel the superiority of our firearms to their spears and tomahawks. We have had substantial proof of the efficiency of this plan where we have as wild characters, in every sense of the word, to deal with as you have there. I mean the Veddas,* armed with bows and arrows, spears and axes. Mrs. Grey and I were reading through the distri- bution of the Company once elected to accompany Colonel Arthur in the pursuit of the Black River Gentlemen, and notice that your name does not appear as an individual in command of a party. I assure you we were most anxiously looking for it, but perhaps you were otherwise- employed by the Colonel's orders. I was rejoiced to find the name of an old friend mentioned as being in command— Darcy Wentworth** of the 73rd, an old and sincere friend of mine, and of my brother- French's. We spent many days' and nights' hardship together, during the Randram's Rebellion, and a more indefatigable officer I never had the opportunity of serving with. I hope you will call on him and make yourself known to him. I have not the smallest doubt that whatever service lies in his power *he will be most happy to render to you and your family. Tell him I visited his old friend at Gonegadda and saw the Inmate, who resided there with him. He is well but the Fort is in a state of dilapidation.*

*Should either duty or pleasure take you to Sydney, you may- meet Cap- tain Rossi, who, when I was in the Isle of Granu*** was most kind and friendly to me. He was formerly of the first Ceylon. I understand he is the Chief Mag- istrate of Sydney. I regret I am not acquainted with any other person in your Colony. It is time now my dear Humphrey, to render an account of myself, and I think the most important part must appear foremost. To be explicit, I must tell you that I found a widower's life anything but agreeable, especially in this cold region, so thought it not amiss to take to myself a second wife, Miss Anne Cavendish. Mrs. Grey is a young Woman, a little advanced of seven- teen, highly accomplished, both in music and drawing, and is considered handsome. I am sure your wife would take great pleasure in her society.*

I was appointed to a Company on November the 29th., but in consequence of there being only three companies vacant in the Regiment, my seniors, Foster and McConochy were appointed commanders to two and the other was given out of the Regiment to an officer on half pay, but at the same time, I received a letter from Lord Fitzroy Somerset by direction of Lord Hill that, should another similar vacancy occur I should be appointed to it. Since which I have been appointed from January 1830 and will no doubt be con- firmed in it. Mrs. Greys and my intention, after my confirmation, is to proceed to V.D.L. where, with the blessing of God and your kind assistance and advice, we hope to spend the rest of our lives in peace happiness and prosperity. Previous to this, I must hear every particular from you and what we can take with us. There is nothing that cannot be procured here, agricultural implements, wearing apparel, furniture of the nicest description also glass and china.

He then added a few family items as "William and Basil are with the 56th" and another page of general gossip and wound up with many affectionate mes- sages to his brother and family.

Letters were serious matters in those days and not to be scrambled through. It was amusing and a little confusing the way Richard referred to his own and his brother's wife as Mrs. Grey He gained promotion in the army and stayed on in Ceylon so he and his wife never did come "to pursue peace, happiness and pros- perity in V.D.L."[1]

Humphrey receives a letter from his brother Richard Gray, Captain 1st Ceylon Regiment who according to the family diary married Anne Cavendish daughter of Cavendish of the Ordinance Department. They had one son. Although this appears by his own account in his correspondence to have been his second marriage. In the letter Richard refers to the Veddas* the indigenous people of Sri Lanka, who, like the Abo- rigines in VDL, were also fighting the British Empire for their very survival. 'The Black River Gentlemen' referred to were located in the central part of Tasmania. It is more likely the Grey family would have settled on the Northern Midlands Nation land.

---

[1] ** The story of Darcy Wentworth Jnr (1793-1861) he mentions is quite remarkable and reads like an adventure story. Darcy was born on Norfolk Is- land on 23rd June 1793 to parents Catherine Crowley and D'Arcy Wentworth (Snr). He was sent to England aged nine for formal education and eventually had a suc- cessful military and political career. During his lifetime he was a military officer, magistrate, Inspector of Police, parliamentarian, landholder He lived at the property *Vaucluse* not far from Avoca.

Sources: Ritchie, John *The Wentworths Father & Son*. Melbourne: Mel- bourne University Press, 1997. Liston, Carol. *Sarah Wentworth Mistress of Vaucluse*. Sydney:Historic Houses Trust, 1988.

===

Another well-known name he refers to is Francis Nicholas Rossi (1776- 1851) whose life achievements are detailed in the *Australian Dictionary of Bi- ography* Vol.2 1788-1851.

===

*** The Isle of Granu: Ireland. "Granu" or "Granuweal" is the name of an unlearned, unaesthetic old woman, signifying Mother Ireland. She probably de- rives from the aristocratic Gaelic woman whom the English called Grace O'Malley, a chieftain in the late C16th Connaught, who fought Gaelic neigh- bours and the governors sent by Elizabeth I to pacify the province. (*Walsh Robin, Honorary Associate, School of Modern History, Macquarie University*)

Finally, the William he refers to is their another brother William Gray, Cap- tain 58th Regiment married his cousin Sophia Broomfield. The couple had no offspring.

Peoples of lutrawita
The Greys arrived in the middle of a war between the British Empire and Northern Midlands Nation. More specifically they had been given land grants in an area where the Tyerrernotepanner people had lived for thousands of years. At the beginning there were an estimated 400 – 500 people. After the War there were none. It was a clash of two civilizations, one with nowhere else to go and the other with guns, disease and Protestant Christianity.
Read more in VOLUME TWO BOX NINE: PEOPLE OF THE NORTHERN MIDLANDS NATION, LUTRAWITA.

War and Peace for the Family
Regardless of the political, military and social events swirling around them the primary concern for the family was to protect their children. This is highlighted in Katie's book when she refers to their mother's very real fear and anguish for her children from attacks by Aborigines. Read more in VOLUME TWO BOX TEN: WAR AND SURVIVAL 1829 - 1832

Molding a new way of life
The brutal war with the Aborigines was now over for the Europeans living in Avoca. The British had won. Their victory was absolute, decisive and final: leaving only silence in the surrounding hills and valleys. The new inhabitants were now safe on their freshly claimed land to live and transplant a different cultural identity on the Island.
Read more in VOLUME TWO BOX ELEVEN: A NEW WAY OF LIFE BEGINS

Moving again

Figure 8 Rockford by Richard Chuck 2017

At last one fine day, the family mounted their bullock dray and set off on the long plodding three miles an hour eighty mile journey to Avoca and this could not even be quickened by the Bullockees using their usual forceful language! They had been solemnly warned that with ladies aboard they could say nothing stronger than "Git up, git up, you beauties," to a moderate cracking of stock whips.

The journey was very entertaining for the children. Each night was spent in a different place in a rough, clean hotel. When there was none enroute Captain James would take them to the home of an earlier settler who would give them a most kindly pleasant welcome and was eager for any news of the Old

Country. The host might take the men of the party around his farm and explain colonial methods of working it.

It was some days before James was able to point out to the excited fam- ily the boundaries and roof-tree of Rockford where an equally excited and delighted family welcome from William, his wife and children awaited them. William had had several rooms built for a temporary home for them and Ellen had supplied beds and bedding and a few comforts. She told them to apply to her for anything they needed. The furniture and china bought at Rio was already installed. There were generous stacks of wood for the big, open fireplaces and once they were lit the family felt they were at home at last. They had been there for two years before the Eastbourne was cleared and fenced and a comfortable stone house lined all through with beautiful unpainted cedar was built. Almost luckily for the early set- tlers a ship bringing a load of cedar had been wrecked in the Tamar and its cargo had been sold for a farthing a foot.

Consequently many of the early homes had beautiful paneled doors, fine stair- cases and narrow inside shutters of Cedar hinged in several pleated pieces, while outside were the stronger heavier ones built in case of bushrangers' attack. It was not hard to get convict labourers, quite a number of whom were skilled men who, if under merciful employers, took a pride in their craftsmanship.

An early building on Eastbourne, the barn, quite probably reflected the need for protection rather than refinement. The family were attacked by Aboriginals and Bushrangers on several occasions and the barn was clearly designed for that purpose with only two very small slits high up on the side of the building. Its construction is rough, solid and built with expediency while the stable appears to have come later and may be made from cleaner cut stone, measured and more care taken in its design and construction.

There is a small cottage closer to the river, the front of which appears to be very old indeed and may have housed some of the family before the construction of the main homestead in 1834. Humphrey went on to acquire more land and properties through his life in- cluding an allocation of 1130 acres in 1838 as well as *Frogmore* and *Woodmount*, formally known as *Mona Vale* at Evandale. This property, he gave to Elizabeth.

The Greys settled happily at Eastbourne. There was so much to learn in their new life. It was impossible to buy many needed things and many months passed before ships returned with orders sent. The girls learnt to spin and weave materials for clothes and beautifully designed linen table cloths and napkins were made which lasted for generations.

Sometimes tragedies would happen, as when two young maids carried a tub full of house linen to the river (the only water supply) to rinse them. A sudden unexpected current swept it out of their reach—a terrible loss of sheets and towels, for they were never seen again.

The elder girls had to spend an hour or two daily getting the young ones to practise reading and writing and learning to recite. Their mother had de- cided to wait until they reached their new home before engaging a tutor for music and French but there were so many new ideas to absorb.

Catherine loved reading but Margaret was her mother's great compan- ionand helped to receive the almost daily visitors. At that time there were quite a number of unattached young settlers in the district in search of a wife so though Margaret was only sixteen her arrival caused quite a stir. Besides that dashing young officers of the 68th Regiment now stationed at Avoca were always find- ing a reason to drop in.

Margaret's diary told of one very persistent suitor, whom she evidently did not look upon with much favour. June 18th. R. W. called to-day. June 20th. R. W. dined with us

June 22nd. R. W. brought his gig and requested me to drive with him. I was too busy. The Old Lady went instead.

June 24th. R.W; called to ask would I care to walk down and see the river in flood. I went, but took Henry with me!

June 27th. R.W. again. This time he brought a little boy with him—an ex- cuse. June 29th. R. W. came to say he was going to town. Had we any com- mission for him?

June 30th. R. W. returned. He brought us some new books.

Humphrey Junior was very fond and proud of Margaret but he teased her, "We hoped to have a flagstone path to our front door, not one of broken hearts." She was very tender-hearted and her eyes filled with tears so Humph- rey comforted her. "Never mind Margaret. Bear up, I hear that Mr. L. and four sisters, are arriving next month." This was true and Margaret soon realised how quickly fancies may roam. Her Father had automatically got into the habit of saying to aspiring young suitors who came asking his per- mission to make their addresses to her, "No, no, we wish Margaret to decide for herself. Her hap- piness comes before everything."

There were six men to every one girl at that time! Margaret's diary spoke of many callers

— Captain Vicary (the C.O.), W.T. Talbot, Willis, Lambert, Wedge (Surveyor- General), Jennings, Parra- more, Franks, Sutherland, Batman (explorer of Port Phillip) who rode his black horse over the river to ask the ad- vice of Major William. Occasionally,

Many of the names mentioned here are well known characters in early Tasmanian history and eas- ily located through library and internet searches. Each one has a unique and fas- cinating story of their own. Those mentioned are: Cap- tain Vicary (the C.O.), W. T. Talbot, Willis, Lambert, Wedge (Surveyor-General), Jennings, Parramore, Suth- erland, Franks, Batman and Simeon Lord from Bona Vista.

when possible, ladies would accompany their husbands and then the journal recorded: "We had a most enjoyable evening, a large party and a great deal of fun."

There were few outside excitements but life was never dull. People dropped in for breakfast, lunch or dinner and hostesses thought nothing of an unexpected arrival such as, "Mr. Cathcart arrived when we were at break- fast." After that meal, morning prayers, for which the entire household assembled, were held. On Sundays, since there was no church to attend, a sermon was read. There was a good deal of feudal feeling. Not only the owners but the workmen took pride in achievement.

Sometimes a whole family would arrive needing a night's rest on the way to their future home. That is why so many four-posters were in use. Mamma and the children would occupy one, while Papa joined the other men in a shake- down. It was impossible in those days of floating population and elastic hospitality to provide a room for each person but the newcomers quickly grasped the situation and were grateful for shelter and rest. Clearing the land and fencing occupied most of the time at first so it was not till some years later that owners had time to build man- sions of forty or fifty rooms. They enjoyed these till another turn of the wheel of Fate caused domestic workers to vanish and the beautiful Georgian houses, became "white elephants" and hospitality almost died.

Dan Falkiner

In 1830 workers seemed to welcome visitors as much as their employers did.

4 Margaret Grey curtesy of Brian Jacobs.

One visitor came for two weeks on his way to his own allot- ment but stayed for two years, finally leaving with his hosts' ex- postulation, "Why go? You know we like having you!" As soon as the horses could be brought out there were riding parties every year and picnic races. Many of the settlers were musical and if one were lucky enough to possess a harpsichord the whole evening would be spent singing songs.

Several young Irishmen had delightful voices. One, Daniel Falkiner, the son of an old Rector in Tipperary had come out to seek a fortune and provide for his three young sisters. He was highly educated and more fit for literary than farming work but he found more scope for the latter in V.D.L. He was far from strong and the doctors had advised him to do outside not inside work and he did his best to tackle it. His neighbours would see him, *The Odyssey* in hand, ploughing the crookedest furrow. Sometimes they went to his aid for he was a general favourite. He was always grate- ful, admiring their superior skill, and he was always ready to do a good turn for anyone. Dan could made characters from Dickens or Thackeray seem alive and real. Children and animals adored him and so the Greys always enjoyed his spending an evening with them singing or discussing literature.

Two of his sisters soon married and the third was no more practical than he so their home, though happy, often looked neglected. When this sister was seventeen she married and went to Victoria. He buried himself more in his books, looked untidy and let his hair grow too long!

> Daniel Richard Falkiner of Co- Tipperary, Ireland and Up- lands Tas: Falkner, son of Falkner Recorder of titles Dub- lin. Children: Three Alice, Kate and Humphrey, Richard and John William (FNB)

> Celebrations
> Margaret met Daniel Richard Falkner, a rather shy, diffident man more comfortable with books and poetry than the practicalities of life. They were married on 27th February 1838 and Humphrey and Kate were soon to welcome their first grandchild, Alice Kate into the world on the 26th Oct 1839. The couple had three children: Alice Kate = John Robertson Humphrey, Richard = Marian O'Connor, John William unmarried. It should be noted that the present O'Connor family living at Benham are descended from the marriage of Humphrey and Marian.

He, Dan, knew all about R.W.'s pursuit of Margaret but evidently Margaret was tired of it so put a stop to it by announcing that she would marry another settler. But this engagement did not last long. "He" was inclined to lay down the law and prefaced most decisions with the words, "I have decided" and seemed to have little interest in her wishes. Accustomed as she was to her gentle father and chivalrous young brother, this attitude surprised and shocked her and she gave him his congé.

It was at that time that R.W. came to ask Dan's help and sympathy. Dan promised to do all he could to help. He knew that if she accepted R.W. she would have a pleasant even luxurious life. He himself thought of her as an evening star beyond the reach of ordinary mortals like himself. When she was worried he thought of her as a moss-rose, surrounded by wasps! R.W. was a different matter, slightly unexciting perhaps but kindness and security itself. He had told Dan how elusive he had found the lady and implored Dan to speak for him. He said, "You see, she has found that her engagement was a mistake, so now I may have a chance." With his ready sympathy Dan said, "Of course I will do what I can, old fellow."

Next morning standing before his mirror in his white, frilly shirt, riding trousers and long shining boots Dan tried to bring his dark, unruly locks to order and not to notice the sadness of his dark-lashed, hazel eyes. He had no vanity and did not realize their beauty. His one thought was how mad he had been to make such a promise.

Dan never shirked his fences nor broke a promise so he swallowed a cup of coffee, put on his tall beaver, a two-caped waisted fawn coat and a blue scarf and went off soberly to whistle to his horse. It came whinnying with pleasure, accepted a lump of sugar and stood quietly to be saddled.

By way of consolation Dan tucked *The Odyssey* in his pocket and rode off quietly for a few miles, though not singing as usual. But he seemed to hear his horse's hooves beating out—"the sooner the better, the sooner over, the better," so he shook up the reins and arrived at Rockford gate in a canter, and there tied up his horse. He did not go to the stables as he did not mean to linger. Out in the garden he saw Margaret herself in a green muslin frock, white stockings and black sandals. She was carrying a shady leghorn hat and looked fresh and sweet. She was gathering flowers and came smiling to the gate, "Why, Dan, you are an early visitor. Have you come to breakfast? Is everything all right?"

He took her hand and spoke abruptly, "Oh, Margaret, it is you I have come to see! I promised Rod that I would. He is such a good fellow and would do anything for you and he has been given your father's permission to speak. Won't you listen to him?" Margaret's eyes were dancing and her cheeks grew pinker as his grew whiter and to his surprise she actually laughed as she said, "No, Dan, no. I will not. I could not. Don't you know that a man should speak for himself, not for others?" Dan was so astounded, he could not speak. His one thought was; *She does not mean, nor know, what her word simply.*

But she had turned her back on him and had gone down into the sloping garden and was examining a bush. He followed her quickly took her by the shoulder and turned her to face him saying, "You can't mean it! You don't really mean what you are saying. You are the loveliest girl in the world and I have nothing, nothing to give you!" Her face was quite serious and very sweet as she answered, "You have yourself Dan and that to me is everything." Dan gasped and flung his arms around her and kissed her. Then he took her hand saying, "Let us find your father."

The parents were not as surprised as was expected. Margaret had given herself away not long before. She had come to her father with an unusual request for a girl of those days. She had asked if she might join the two Humphreys and Dan when they read from the Latin poets. On being asked why, she had said, "Humphrey is rather fond of Latin, and I thought we might enjoy it together." She became pink when her father said, "A kind sisterly thought but there is no need for you to worry, my dear, Humphrey can get Dan or myself to read with him. You know we all enjoy it. Stick to your French, music and dancing. That is all a girl needs." A little later he was heard singing, "Amo, amass, I love a lass," until Mrs. Grey, with amused eyes, begged him to desist, saying he was out of tune! After their engagement was announced Margaret took the reins but in such a happy tactful way that Dan never realised, it. She was naturally inclined to be a little managing and his delicacy and need of care aroused her maternal instincts strongly. Her father insisted on an engagement of not less than six months. Dan was burning with impatience to make his house and garden more worthy of her so he rose at daylight and worked till dark and began to look so thin and tired that she would ride over with Humphrey and a gardener. They would all work for a while then Margaret would get Dan into the house to suggest improvements.

Her father saw the effort they were both making and recognised her happiness lay with Dan and so though he wished she could have an easier life he found several ways to help them. It was not difficult to get labourers and give Dan help with his sheep, and Mrs. Grey heard of a strong, healthy woman to do their housework. Margaret and her mother were busy getting extra furniture and furnishings and making everything fresh, much to Dan's admiration.

The brick house was not large but comfortable and was built around a square courtyard, the living-rooms and bedrooms in front the kitchen and dairies down one side and on the other, stables and room for grooms. The fourth side was a solid brick wall whose heavy gate was locked each night in case of unwelcome invaders.

5 Wickford property, Longford. By Glover, John Richard- son, 1790-1868

Happiness and Tragedy Wickford[iii]

After Margaret was married she used her capable brain not only to run her home well but also to help Dan with the farm which prospered accordingly. Under her pretty curls was a shrewd, observant mind and though she did none of the manual work she would encourage Dan to discuss with Humphrey and other men what seasonal work had to be done and she made helpful notes in her journal mixing news of her neighbours with farm items.

Mrs. L. was 'confined of a son to-day, stands next to, Barley sown to-day or Cow was killed. On one occasion she wrote, I got a great shock to-day, I saw an express coming over the lawn, but it was only for Dan to attend the in- quest at Campbell Town. It was on the poor hawker, murdered near the Tiers, whose horse and cart were stolen. Another entry ran, We joined the family at East-bourne, and then we all rode over to Grey Fort, where we found the family, in great dismay. Captain James had gone to Port Dalrymple. Mrs. Grey was far from well. The servants had got drunk and had taken the baby to the bush."

The years slipped by busily and happily. On winter evenings Dan would read his beloved books aloud to Margaret while she sewed for their two small sons. Sometimeshe would sing for her and the house was full of music. He was anxious that the boys should inherit the culture that was handed down to him so when they reached five or six years he began teaching them Latin verbs and over and over again he made them repeat his family's motto *Fortuna favente* (By Favour of For- tune) and told them they must not forget it. It was naturally a quiet life and their fortune had its ups and downs but there was always hope and content-

6 Figure 10 by Richard Chuck

ment at Prospect, their home. How could there be anything else with Margaret at the reins with such a willing team to drive?

Then without warning disaster came. She was dressing to go out for a ride, put her hand into her riding boot and was stung by a poisonous spider. Everything possible was done. Dan cut and sucked the bite. A groom galloped to Avoca for Dr. Brock, and another went to Eastbourne. But nothing did any good. She lived for only two days. By the time Catherine and her father arrived she was past knowing them. She had smiled at Dan and slipped into uncon-sciousness from which she never awoke.

Dan was stunned. He had to be aroused to be with the children and to see to the farm animals. He seemed drained of all thought. It ended by Cath- erine and her father taking everything in hand, closing the house and getting Dan to appoint his most reliable worker as overseer and then the whole fam- ily went to East-bourne. There they stayed for some time, then Dan told them he could not face the thought of returning to Prospect, which was sold. He could not settle in the country so took his younger boy to town where he would see to his education but the elder Humphrey, named after his grandfather, went to Hobart to be with Eliza-beth and go to boarding school with her boys. A few years later Elizabeth, who thought the boys should all have a home, found and engaged a capable house-keeper for them and they all went back to the country to live at Frogmore a property bequeathed to Humphrey by his grandfather, who had not lived long after Margaret.

The house there was not very comfortable and when Humphrey wished to marry, he was told by the father of the lady of his choice that he must find a better house. He was quite willing so they sold Frogmore and bought a well-built beautiful home Wickford some miles away and settled there.

There are two possible culprits responsible for Margarets demise which are **Funnel Web Spider** and the **Redback Spider**.

Margaret and Daniel Falkiner

Margaret Helena 1807-22 December 1860   Daniel R Falkiner d31 Jan 1868 married on 27 Feb 1838

Alice Kate = John Robertson d1902	Humphrey Richard = Marian O'Connor daughter of Arthur O'Connor of Connerville. They lived at Wickford Estate Longoford	John William unmarried d14th Nov 1927

Herbert Falkiner b1863 = May Windsor	Maud	Charles (Twin to Helena) b 1872	Helena Margaret (Twin to Charles) b 1872 = ? Leeming	John Percival

	Katherine Margaret (Ketha)	Millicent Louisa	Arthur O'Connor	Eileen O'Connor	Marian (May) = Guy Mackinnon second son of Alan Mackinnon Montford Longford

Donald Herbert Windsor b1897	Gordon John b1902		Molly Falkiner b July 1913	Arthur Guy b1st May 1916	Dorthy Ralston b 1919	Alan McLean

Figure 11 Eastbourne by Richard Chuck

Education

When Margaret was married, the Greys had been living at Eastbourne for three years. Mrs. Grey was anxious for the girls to continue their education and was able to get a cultured, elderly man to ride over from Avoca two or three times a week and keep up their interest in French, music and literature. Henrietta was to go to a good boarding school as soon as one could be heard of but Lysbeth was considered too young to leave home. She had to read daily to the girls but was sent out to play when the tutor came.

Mrs. Grey often sat with the girls while he talked of the countries he had visited and in which their friend William Talbot, with his tutor was then travelling. William was doing the "Grand Tour" as was customary for young men of those days to finish their education and to give them more knowledge of life before settling down. He was a great friend of Humphrey Jun. and wrote him descriptive letters which they all read. On one occasion they had just received a long account of William's visit to Spain. The girls' tutor knew Madrid well and added to the description. It all sounded so romantic, dark-eyed senoritas looking from balconies over moonlit courtyards while their lovers serenaded them to the soft sound of lutes. Even Mrs. Grey sighed unconsciously in unison with the girls. It was all so far away from pioneering. Suddenly from behind an armchair in the corner, burst a whirl-wind. Lysbeth scarlet-cheeked, said, "William never did. He doesn't know how!" She was a little jealous. She knew him well, as he had often come to Eastbourne and she had no intention of allowing that he might be interested in any Spanish beauty. She need not have worried her child heart. His one thought was how soon he could return to Catherine!

Recovering from Lysbeth outburst Mrs. Grey as calmly as she could for she was longing to laugh said, "Kate, take Lysbeth to the nursery. She must stay there now.

She knows she should not be here!" The culprit went off with Kate, who was also finding it hard not to laugh. The nursery door was shut and she was left without a word.

Lysbeth resignedly got her dolls out of the cup- board. Jemima and Bridget were very prim ladies indeed, made of wood, with coal black hair and painted eyes. Their limbs were stiff. She had no love for them, but dressed them propped them on the table and began to read aloud the *Fairchild Family*, a book much approved of by parents of those days.

It was so intensely moral and she loathed such a disgustingly virtuous family.

> The children's book referred to here is *The His- tory of the Fairchild Family* 1881. 1842 and 1847 by Sherwood Mary Martha (1775-1851). Although it seems unlikely the children would have read Struwwelpeter(*Shockheaded Peter*) as it was not pub- lished in English until around 1848 but did eventually become favorite children's book for many years. It is more likely to have been read by the next generation.

There was only one chapter from which Lysbeth got some enjoyment. The Fairchild family had been left to play in the garden under the care of an elderly manservant, John, while their parents were in town. They had been given strict instructions not to leave the garden. Somehow a pig got in and they chased it into a neighbour's place where they had been forbidden to enter. The neigh- bour saw them and invited them to have cake and cider. Did they refuse nicely and leave? No, they took it all and wandered down the road where later on John found them in the ditch quite drunk!

After reading this harrowing tale she looked seriously at Jemima and Brid- get and said, "Now you two, let that be a lesson to you. Do as you are told and do not go to the cider press when we are in bed!" Then she sighed deeply and feeling lonely and disgruntled threw the *Fairchild Family* into a corner after which she turned to another well-known child's book *Struwwelpeter* (*Shock- headed Peter*) which had a far more thrilling way of inculcating morals. Each page was vividly illustrated and drove home the facts and results of Badness!

There was Fidgety Phil who never sat still. He was on a high chair at the table, rocking backwards and forwards and when he lost his balance he grabbed the cloth and the dishes flew everywhere. Opposite him were two horrified par- ents denouncing him in plain language. Another page showed a rude boy mocking a black man and calling him "Nigger". Immediately from nowhere ar- rived an avenger who took him by the hair and dropped him into the inkpot!

Poor Lysbeth! She had read all about the boy who wouldn't eat his dinner and about the one who walked into the sea. She was bored and missed Henny who was away on a short visit, when in walked Catherine looking charming in her dark green habit, scarlet waistcoat, lace ruffles and little three- cornered feathered hat. In a glance, Kate took in everything but said nothing. Lysbeth very red had rushed to pick up the *Fairchild Family* and said "Oh Kate, I was just going to put the girls to bed. I don't think Jemima likes the *Fairchilds*. She is sick of them and threw them into a corner."

Kate, whose back was turned said, "Whatever would Mama think of her tantrums?" and as the dolls were hastily undressed and put to bed she added, "I was really wondering if Lysbeth would like to go for a ride?" She was almost pulled over when two little arms hugged her and the excited response came,

"Oh Kate you darling. She would love it and so will Goldie," [her pony]. Then Kate dressed her till she was a miniature of herself and putting on yellow gauntlet gloves they went to the front door to find the groom waiting to mount them and ready to ride with them to Rockford.

It was not considered safe to allow young girls to ride unattended. They might meet Aborigines, rough men, convicts in the charge of soldiers or even bushrangers, so an armed groom always rode near them. Some years later a young friend of Catherine's, Elizabeth Youl, rode down the road with her. They were unattended when suddenly from bushes in front burst some ragged men shouting, `"Halt!"But

> Martin Cash (1808 – 1877) was infa- mous for his antics at the time and known as the Gentleman Bushranger. While bushrangers have attained acertain sta- tus in recent times, in reality many were desperate, dangerous and ruthless men. This is illustrated well by the story of the murder at Simeon Lord's home from the Colonial News. (1853, January 29) The Maitland Mercury and Hunter River Gen- eral Advertiser (NSW: 1843-1893), p4
> Read more in Volume Two box twelve: bushrangers, theft and murder

it was Martin Cash* in charge of them and though the girls got a shock no harm was done. He merely asked them their names and destination, did not touch them nor their horses   but just said, "Ride on ladies," restraining a man who looked troublesome. The girls bore the names of families known to treat their convict employees well. Some em- ployers, unnecessarily severe and probably unaccustomed to authority, would send a man to be flogged for quite small offences and when the bushrangers could retaliate they did, robbing him of food, money and valuables. The Greys like certain other families in the district were never robbed nor attacked by them though quite unknowingly they came into contact with them more than once.

Bushrangers

Figure 12 by Richard Chuck

On one occasion Humphrey Sen. was riding down the road on which settlers of all types either rode or drove in bullock drays. This time he met a well-dressed man on a beautiful horse which was not unusual as settlers nearby imported such horses. This time with his love of horseflesh Humphrey rode slowly admiring the animal. The stranger halted opposite him

Figure 13 Figure 18 Bona Vista SIR RALPH WHISHAW 1966 'Whishaw Collection' Tasmanian Archive and Heritage Office

raised his hat and enquired in a pleasant voice, "I wonder sir if you would be so kind as to direct me to some of the properties near. I do not know the district and I particularly wish to call on—" He named five. This was not an unusual request in a newly settled country so Humphrey did not hesitate. He asked no questions but gave directions as well as could then after a few pleasant remarks they parted. Humphrey thought no more of it then but he did the next day when the police called to ask if bushrangers had been there and told him that five places had been robbed. They were the places he had mentioned! Was it a coincidence? He didn't mention the attractive stranger.

Humphrey had an understanding way of making men feel his authority without unhappiness. Perhaps his experience with soldiers in his youth helped him. Some of his men spent their lives working for him and regarded him with affection and respect. Years after he died his little great-grand-daughter spoke to two of his old grooms who had been pensioned off and were living in Launceston. They were both over four-score but they made a yearly pilgrim- age, walking to the Avoca cemetery to see again where the old master and his family lay. It took more than a week for this journey.

Near to Eastbourne was an owner unaccustomed to authority who by way of making his workers feel his importance was very severe with them and was hated. He'd often sent them to be flogged so they planned revenge and freedom. One of his grooms joined others and visited the Avoca police station when the men were at their evening meal, stole their horses and rode them to Mr. Simeon Lord's. Here the family were at late dinner and Miss Isobel the petted daughter wore a valuable necklace with earrings to match. Suddenly galloping horses and shots were heard near the house and Mr. Lord looking out exclaimed, "Bushrangers!"

Miss Isobel pulled off her jewels and sat on them but the leading bushranger was equally quick. Having noticed that every-one except Isabel had risen in an agitated manner he first made the men "hands up", stand against the wall facing his gun, while one of his men went through their pockets. Then they searched the house for food and money. This done they went to the stables to secure the beautiful blood horses to have everything ready for a quick get-away. The bushranger then said, "Now then Miss Isobel stand up." She did not dare disobey. He took the jewelry, saying, "Thank you" then joined the others. They rode the beautiful horses, driving the heavier po- lice ones before them for a time.

As they went quietly down the road they came to Eastbourne on a fine summer morning about 5 a.m. Humphrey, an old man, now was out in his garden near the road. They halted saying, "Good morning sir." He didn't recognise them but knew the horses and said, "Good morning men you are out early exercising the horses!"

To this they answered "Yes sir Bushrangers were at 'Bona Vista' last night and we are hunting for them." "Oh" he said, "unfortunate— well—if you want some breakfast go around to the kitchen," which they did and took nothing but the breakfast! Some hours later the police arrived. They had not missed the horses until a boy from "Bona Vista" arrived on foot and then the hunting for them and having to find others delayed them.[iv] So it was noon before they reached Eastbourne and by that time the bushrangers were far away. The Greys could not help feeling glad they had not known. They knew Mr. Lord to be a hard cruel man and were sorry for anyone at his mercy.

> OUTRAGES BY BUSHRANGERS, — A correspondent at Campbell Town has furnished the following startling intelligence. On Thursday morning two men, armed with double barrelled guns, pistols, and revolvers, and who are supposed to be the men who lately robbed the "Half-way House," went to the house of Mr. Simeon Lord, Bona Vista, near Avoca : Mr. Lord was from home. The fellows bailed up thirty men, including the district constable of Avoca, the watchhouse-keeper, and another constable. The watchhouse-keeper was shot dead, and the constable severely wounded. From the district constable they took a gold watch, and over £20 in money. There were at Mr. Lord's at the time several young ladies, who were all summoned together. The house was ransacked, and the robbers took possession of between £100 and £200 in money, several watches, and articles of jewellery. They then ordered Mr. Frank Lord to provide for them two of the best horses in the stable, and mounting these, they proceeded to the inn kept by Mr. Duxbury, at Stoney Creek, where they bailed up about twelve men, including two unarmed constables. They com-

Letters from Home

By 1832 long crisscrossed letters of thick paper gilt-edged if written by a lady, arrived from the family in Ireland. The writing was very fine and straight and when finished the whole letter was folded and sealed to form an envelope which were not in use at that time. There were no stamps on the addressed side but probably a crown and "ship's letter" in one corner. In another would be *Obliged by Major Russell* or some friend. The letter always seemed the result of an unhurried day's work and expressed everything in the most flowery terms. No item of possible interest was forgotten and capital letters were scattered profusely, not being used as we use them, but to emphasis the writer's news. Catherine had one from her cousin, Alice:

My own, dear Catherine

Again do I resume an occupation rendered most Delightful to me, as it communicated Pleasure to those Valued relations in a Foreign land, of whom Remembrance is Cherished with fond Affection by all members of the Mallow circle. I daresay you got my letter which I sent by Mr. Bingham. I received your Wished-for letter on St. Patrick's Day last and take this Opportunity of sending this letter by Major Russell, who is taking his Family and twelve children with him. Sam, the Eldest, has gone into the Army, so will not be with them. Martha, the eldest Daughter, is a very nice girl.

She speculates on getting a husband by going. I heard that a Gentle- man, named Anderson, has left Kilkenny for the purpose of becoming a cousin of Mine. Not knowing to a certainty if it were true or not, I made enquiries as to his character, and hear it is most Exceptionable. I often see your cousin Emily. She is a very Nice girl and is both Low and Stout.

John Quain spent two months after Xmas with us, after being in Germany for two years. You must know he is achieving his early ambition to be a lawyer. The Hutchinsons have gone to live in London, where James is performing the most wonderful Cures, and is patronised by the most Eminent of the Faculty!

Dan was bound to a Doctor, and had served some of his time, when the servant and he had an Argument, which enraged Dan to strike him; for fear of being punished by the Law, he went to America, where he became Editor of a paper, but he could make Nothing of that! He then went on the Stage where his Vocal Abilities were not less Admired and Applauded than his Elocutory Powers. He was not long a Theatrical when his Master made up the Breach with him. He has since finished his term, and is an Assistant Surgeon in the Army.

We are going on in the same old way. We have had neither an Addition, nor, thank God, a Diminution in our Family Circle. Papa, praise be to the Omnipotent Being, Who presides in all things, enjoys Perfect Health and Mama too, has that great Blessing. "Little" Johnny is no longer a Candidate for that title as he is' fully six feet high.

I intend this day, setting out for Galway to spend a month. William Quain has a Perpetual Curacy in the county Tyrone. He is looked up to, as if he were an angel in Human form. We hear from him occasionally. He made me a promise to unite me in marriage! It must be to a Protestant, but I have not provoked him yet.

Every person in this establishment unites most sincerely in love to you. Write and mention particularly how you all are in health and if there is hope that we shall meet this side of the Grave.

Adieu, dear. That is the fond wish of your devoted cousin, ALICE

Figure 14 Barn at Eastbourne

Eastbourne homestead had not long been finished and the family comfortably installed when Catherine at last had leisure to make a full response to Alice's letter. She gave an account of an incident which showed the character of the girl of the day. She might have the fashionable "vapours" or swoon at the sight of blood, but in a real emergency, she would be ashamed not to rise to the occasion, so Kate, aged fifteen, wrote to Alice;

My dear Cousin,

There is so much to tell you, but to-day, it will be chiefly about yesterday's doings. Margaret and Lysbeth were at Rockford, and Papa and Mama went for them. Papa had been able to get a comfortable equipage and to buy a pair of matching bays from Mr. Lord, who imports them. It was a lovely day and they left early, to make the best of it.

Martha and Biddy were busy in the house. Barnes and the stable boy were turning out the stables. All seemed well, and Humphrey went off to the Marsh, a mile away, to see to some sheep. Henny and I were gardening and meant later to go inside and enjoy Scott's poems, which Uncle had sent to us. Suddenly there were shrieks and Biddy came flying to us!, saying, "Miss Kate, Miss Kate, a snake has bitten Barnes and he will die !" You may imagine how we ran and rushed to the courtyard, where we found poor Barnes surrounded by the others, terrified. On the ground near, was a huge black snake, dead, but still writhing. We had all been told that with snake bite, we must Act quickly, so I sent Henny to Martha for a bowl of hot water and clean rags, and told a boy to scrub along.

Biddy was useless. After screaming, she flopped on the ground in a dead faint, of which no one took any notice. Barnes is such a good groom and so obliging. He kept his head, but was very white when I told him to wash his finger in; the bowl. Then I said, "Barnes, you know it cannot be helped. Your finger must be cut off at once." No one said a word. Humphrey was so far away, I knew I had to do it Myself. But I did feel sick. Seeing how deadly pale poor little Henny was, I told her to tell Martha to bring the sharpest chopper and that she must not come out again. She fled. Fortunately, the bite was on his fore-finger. Everyone stood silent when Barnes put it on the block, and using all my Strength, I cut if off, praying inwardly that I might not hurt his thumb.

It was all right, and what do you think our wise little Henny did? Of her own accord, she ran around the house hunting for, and fortunately finding, a clean,

Barnes may have been bitten by either a Tiger Snake or a Low- land Copperhead, both of which are venomous and can kill.

Lowland Copperhead

Tiger Snake

new Cobweb and with some Sugar gave it to Martha. We washed the wound and put on the Web and Sugar and that stopped the bleeding. Martha had just bandaged Barnes' hand and wrist when there was the Sound of Galloping and Humphrey, his horse dripping and gasping, dismounted and rushed to us. He called, "Kate, are you all right?" Then looked at Barnes and told a boy to walk him up and down, while he went to the house to get him some Brandy and made him drink it. He also said they must hunt around and see if there were any more snakes about.

Meanwhile, knowing all was well, I went to the Parlour to Henny, and sat down. I have heard of ladies Swooning, but never thought I would! But I did feel Queer, Then Martha came in and pushed my head on to my knees, then said I must lie down. She returned in a few minutes with a tray, teapot and cups and made us both drink some tea. It had such a Funny taste, I Suspect strongly that some of Barnes" brandy had got into it by mistake! We felt better and then she made us eat some lovely hot scones, "swimming in butter." She had just made them when the Commotion began. She said Barnes was all right now and Mr. Humphrey was making him rest and then was coming in to have scones with us.

When he did, he told us what a Terrible Fright he had had. A stable boy on his pony had galloped to him, shouting, "Mr. Humphrey, Mr. Humphrey, Barnes has been bitten by a snake, and Miss Kate is cutting his hand off."

Humphrey never rode such a race as he did then. He was sure I would try to do Something, but could I? He was terrified in case he should not be in time, and then he said, "I am proud of my sisters, only for you, Barnes might have died." We told him that we could not have; done it without Martha, and he said,

"Thank God for good old Martha." And went off to tell her how pleased Mama and Papa would be with her.

He said he would not leave the house and we must rest. Soon after Biddy came weeping, "would we forgive her for being so useless and losing her head?

But she could not bear it. She and Barnes had planned to marry one day, they would never forget what Miss Kate had done for them."

I really Felt we could not talk about it, so told her as we had used all the Cobwebs and there were No More for her to chase, she must go and spend the rest of the day helping to care for Barnes, so she went off, very happy.

Do write soon. I have no more to tell you this time. All the family unite with me in sending loving messages to you and all the others.

Your Affectionate Cousin, KATE.v

Catherine and the Snake

It is an understatement to say the early colonial families had to be self- reliant. This was especially so in relation to their health and medical needs. Each was culturally bound to the medicines of their home land and relied on the folklore and practices of they knew. It was the way it always had been. Doctors in Western culture are a much more recent phenomenon. The few practising in the Colony were mainly employed by the Colonial Medical Service and their main responsibilities related to convicts and the military. Private doctors did not really appear until many years later and even then often found it hard to make a living. Life was precarious and mortality high in the first few years of the Colony even though 'the common childhood infections were absent until the 1830s This was evidenced by Catherine's experience when aged 15 the groom was bit- ten by a snake in the barn at Eastbourne. The letter shows several interesting aspects of the times. The first is, as Dougharty points out the misconception that girls of that era were meek and mild and did little more than needlework and wait to be married. Catherine at 15 is a strong, clear headed individual and one who could take control in a crisis.

The other interesting aspect is the use of cobwebs for the wound. Henny (Henrietta), still a child knew to collect cobwebs without any direction so clearly it was something she had grown up knowing. The use of cobwebs has long been used in many cultures for a variety of uses in medicine but especially so to stop bleeding and clean the wound. It is even mentioned by Shakespeare who refers to the staunching qualities of cobwebs in A Midsummer Night's Dream "I shall desire you of more acquaintance, good master cobweb, If I cut my finger, I shall make bold of you."

Rosari Kingston 2015 refers to its Irish derivation by saying; In Ireland it has been recorded and "can be traced back to a medical manuscript that was transcribed from Latin into Irish by an Irish Liaig, T.Ó Cuinn in 1415. This manuscript is a compilation in Irish of various Latin works that were in gen- eral use by medical people in the middle ages. The principal source of the knowledge therein is the Circa Instans and this has been dated to shortly after 1070 (Murphy, 1991). The Tadhg Ó Cuinn manuscript has this to say about cob- webs." Snakes were completely unknown to the Irish so Catherine must have learned what to in the case of a bite after she arrived in VDL. She knew to take decisive action and did not hesitate in the amputation.

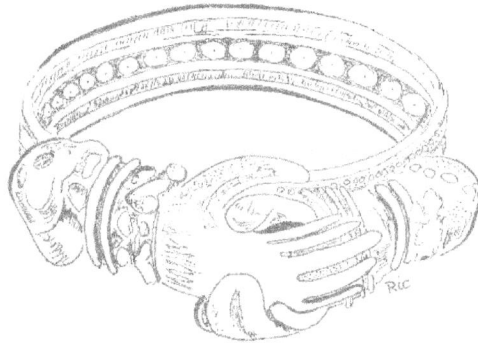

Figure 15 Illustration by Richard Chuck

A Visit from the Governor

Shortly after this Margaret had again gone away for a week's visit when one morning early a boy on horseback clattered noisily over the cobbled courtyard. He brought a note from Major William Gray asking for help in an emergency.

Dear Humphrey,

Mrs. Gray wishes me to ask if you and Kitty would allow Catherine to visit us for a few days. We are expecting a visit from Governor and Suite, in two days' time. They wish to make a survey of the district. [x] .

If it were possible, we should be charmed if you and your wife could accompany Kate, but we know that Humphrey is in Hobart Town and you may not think it wise to leave your home.

"The Old Lady" [his mother] would be so glad of Catherine's support for the occasion. Mrs. Gray is not very well. She would be immensely pleased if you allow Catherine to come, and, of course, we would send the carriage for her.*[xi]

Your affectionate cousin, WILLIAM GREY.

Humphrey took the note to his wife and discussed it before calling Kate. They agreed that, with the elders away it would be unwise to leave the children in charge of the servants. There were so many Aborigines roaming about and a few miles away was a convict settlement. They decided that the visit would be a pleasant experience for Kate so they told her to dress and pack and sent a note to Rockford to relieve Mrs. Gray's mind saying that she would be ready at three 'clock.

Kate had an adaptable nature and would fit in and help. She was highly delighted and the small girls equally so. They went to her room to give advice on packing her sandal- wood box. Lysbeth ideas were practical. She said, "Let's put every- thing that you need on the bed first your kerchiefs, brush and comb, toothbrush," and was interrupted by Henrietta's who did not care for prosaic things "Take your blue French muslin, with blue ribands, and then Kate you will want your pink organdie for the first evening and your silver sandals." Lysbeth went on, "Your riding- habit and boots and will you have your green Gingham** in case you walk in the orchard?" xii "Yes," burst in irrepressible Henrietta again, "you will need your Leghorn and your new riding hat with the green feather."

*"The Old Lady was Anne 'Gray, William and James' mother. Their father was Richard Gray, MD of Birr, Kings County Ireland. She died at Rockfort 27 April1837.
=======================
**In their fluster to prepare Kate for herventure Lysbeth suggests the take her green Gingham with her which is a lightweight plain-woven cot- ton cloth typically checked in white and a bold colour. (Oxford Dictionary online 2015)

They were enjoying themselves thoroughly but suddenly Kate had had enough of them and her mother had come to see what they were doing and banished them to play— Henny saying, "Come on Lysbeth let us play. You can be His Excellency and I will be Kate curtsying to you." Kate laughed and thanked them as they went off.

Punctually at three the old coachman in a low carriage escorted by two young men on horseback arrived. One was William Talbot from Break-O'-Day who was also on a visit to Rockford and the other was Basil, Major William's eldest son aged fourteen. Both came in to pay their compliments to Mrs. Grey but would not linger. The sooner they got away the better. They had to travel slowly and bumpily over unmade roads, and no one knew what dangers lurked there. Henny and Lysbeth saw them start and the last they saw of the children was a picture, Henny stood stiffly, one hand across her chest in imitation of the Governor while Lysbeth coyly acted Catherine, making a deep curtsy.

Kate never forgot that day, such a lovely one. The beauty of the surrounding country the deep blue of the Tiers and the delightful scent of the rain-sprinkled gums impressed her. The two gallant escorts rode as near as safety permitted on each side of the carriage vying with one another in making well-turned compliments, telling any news they could and exchanging gay witty repartee all for Kate's benefit. She tried not to give more

The governor in ques- tion was Col. George Arthur (1784- 1854) was Governor of VDL from May 1824 to Oct 1836. It is doubtful if the evening would have been overly revelrous considering Arthur's black and dower Calvinistic demeanor and disapproval of alcohol.

atten-tion to the debonair William than to her young cousin but it was an effort! Still young as she was she had already a natural sweet- ness and poise so that she survived. William was her brother's great friend and often came to Eastbourne and had heard admiringly of the snake incident.

She arrived at Rockford with even brighter eyes and more glowing cheeks than usually descended from the carriage with the grace taught at her Paris school. William, who had dismounted, quickly assisted her and they received a warm welcome from Major William and the "Old Lady." The very young only daughter of the family had been christened "Frances Anne Talbot Gray," her Godparents being Catherine Grey and Hon William Talbot.

MARRIAGES.

LEDGE—THOMPSON.—On 18th February, at Brunswick Victoria, William Vincent Legge, Esq., Royal Artillery, to Frances Ann Talbot, relict of the late Alex. Thompson, E-q. of Mount Esk, Tasmania, and only daughter of the late Major Gray, 99th Regiment.

Frances grew up to marry twice, the first time to Alexander Thompson. On their honeymoon they visited San Francisco and were there when the Great Fire broke out. He helped in the rescue work and in recognition of this the city presented him with a pair of beautiful golden candelabra. But he was injured, developed pneumonia and died in Nov 1862. Frances returned to Tasmania and in about five years married Colonel Vincent Legge, of Cullenswood. She was then wont to remark, "What a mess I have made of my initials—F. A. T. Legge." But she was a beauty and could afford to jest at herself.*

Editor's note *The book states that Frances Anne Talbot GRAY went to San Francisco on her honeymoon with Alexander THOMPSON & that they were caught up in the Great Fire ultimately leading to Alexander's death & France's remarriage to William Vincent LEGGE several years later. There must be some confusion here as Frances GRAY married Alexander THOMPSON on 17th March 1853, nearly three years after the Great Fire which was the 14th June 1850. (NAME_INDEXES:846289 LINC Tasmania) Although that is not to undervalue his apparent bravery which may well have occurred in a different fire event. He died on the 23rd November 1863.

THOMPSON—On the 23rd November last, at San Francisco, Alexander Thompson, Esq., merchant, of firm Messrs. McKenzie, Thompson, and Co., of that city, and brother of John Thompson, Esq., of this town.

Launceston Examiner Family Notices. (1863, April 23). p. 4 Edition: MORNING She was to re-marry on either the 19th of February 1868 to Colonel Vincent Legge, R.A. was the son of Robert Vincent Legge of *Cullenswood* Tasmania and of Elizabeth Graves, daughter of Captain John Richards La Pinotière R.N of Menheniot, Cornwal England. They were to have two sons and one daughter: Vin- cent; Ellinor (Ellie) Francis Elizabeth; Robert M Flannogan and had one son Ar-thur.(FND) His full name was William Vincent Legge (2nd Sept 1841 – 25th March 1918) and 'was married first, on 1 December 1867 to Frances Anne Talbot (d.1914), widowed daughter of Major W. Gray, of Avoca, second, at Sydney on 3 August 1916 to Kathleen Louisa, daughter of Arthur Cunningham Douglas

of Hobart had a very interesting career which may be reviewed in the Austral- ian.' Dictionary of Biography. Dollery E M Australian Dictionary of Biography Volume 5, (MUP) 1974

LEGGE-THOMPSON.-On 19th February, at Brunswick Victoria, William Vincent Legge, Esq. Royal Artillery to Frances Ann Talbot, relict of the late Alex Thompson, Esq. Mount Esk, Tasmania, and only daughter of the late Ma- jor Gray, 94th Regiment. Launceston Examiner Family Notices. (1868, February 27) p. 4. Children of William Vincent Legge & Frances Anne Talbot GRAY were Vincent Gray de Lappenotiere born 24 Feb 1869 in Columbo, Ceylon 2. Elizabeth Frances Elleanor LEGGE born 7 May 1872 in Galle, Ceylon and 3. Robert William LEGGE born 16 December 1875 in Tricomalee, Ceylon. The latter had a single son named Arthur LEGGE. Jenny Stiles (unpublished).

The Dinner Party

Like most early settlers Mrs. Grey and her husband kept open house and were noted for their hospitality. Many well-known travellers came to their home sure of their welcome. The only drawback to such hospitality was Mrs. Grey's delicate health. She was not very robust and was prone to bad headaches for which a rest in bed was the only solution. The standard of her house-keeping demanded that things should be well done. Most of the servants were rough ex-convicts and needed much training so there was little chance of the mistress relaxing.*

In appearance she was a dainty little lady with a pretty, oval, finely- featured face and sweet eyes. She had a sense of humour and was admired and loved by many friends. She always dressed in stiff rich silk with "real" lace at the neck and wrists. On her head she wore a lace or net cap with lappets reaching from her smooth fine hair to her shoulders.

Kate was delighted to go and stay with her and specially to join in the preparation for a party. She and Mrs. Grey rose early next day and before 6 a.m. were in the kitchen with Cook. Several things were already done. On the cool wired- in underground storeroom shelves rich plum cakes, mince pies, plum puddings waited, also a ham cooked in port wine. When Kate went into the room she was filled with admiration. On the shelves too were cut-glass cups of custard and beautiful green Worcester dishes on which stalked strawberries would be piled and next to them were two fat silver jugs to hold whipped cream. Brandy sauce too must be made.

The housekeeper of 1830 had not dreamt of refrigerators nor even of Mrs. Beeton but many prized and well-tried recipes were handed down from mother to daughter. Until 12.30 Catherine, Mrs. Grey and her staff were fully occupied. They had had a meal and were sent off to rest. The Governor and suite were not expected until 5 p.m. Kate had spent the greater part of the morning making the dinner table beautiful. She had two or three black Wedgwood bowls, filled with lovely pink camelias. The very handsome Georgian silver twinkled on the finely hand-woven linen cloth. A chest of silver had been brought safely from the old home. It had been especially designed in 1801 at the time of the Union of England, Ireland, Scotland and Wales and their emblems were embossed on the handles on each piece.

Acorns were wrought on the spoon bowls, while the rose thistle shamrock and leek were raised on the handles. They were used only on special occasion such as weddings and parties and the Grays hoped to hand them on to their descendants. There were spoons of all shapes and sizes and Kate loved to unpack them and rub them on the soft chamois in which they were rolled. There were goblets of Waterford glass and a Dresden service. Everything sparkled under the light of the Sheffield-plate candelabra. The polished cedar walls and the backs of the mahogany dining chairs shone like pools of water reflecting the flowers and pretty colours. Dinner was at eight o'clock. Then there was no such thing as "afternoon tea." This was instituted by the Duchess

---

* The English convict system needs to be considered in the context of the times. Great Britain was in the midst of massive social, political and economic upheaval from the late 1700s. The Industrial Revolution had transformed the nation from a rural based society to one which created wealth through both agrarian and industrial innovation and brilliant engineering.

of Bedford in 1852 but any of the household was at liberty to visit and enjoy the apple-room. Mrs. Gray firmly believed in the "apple-a-day" theory.

That afternoon the threatened headache became rapidly worse. She fought it until every preparation for the visit had been made. Then knowing that rest was the only cure she went to lie down. By 6.30 it had not abated. The "Old Lady", William's mother, was most concerned and would not leave her, for when she tried to stand she became faint. Finally they sent for Catherine saying, "Catherine dear I am afraid I must ask a great deal of you. Will you act as hostess at the dinner to-night? You can see that I am useless and it would comfort me to know that you will see to everyone's well- being and enjoyment?"

Poor Kate! Her heart jumped and almost failed her. What an ordeal! And she had not made her debut and felt very inexperienced. If only Margaret had been there instead! She flushed and her eyes were full of anxiety but she did not interrupt Mrs. Gray who went on, "You must not feel nervous. Your cousin and William will help you. Remember you will be entertaining gentlemen who will realise your youth and will do everything to help you. "The Major will see that correct wines are served and cook knows how to send the dishes in. I will be glad if you will take another look at the table to see if the silver and glass are adequate. The Major will welcome His Excellency and make my excuses, and will show them to their rooms. You need not hurry. A hostess must appear calm and at her ease and you need not appear till just before dinner when you will meet them all in the drawing-room."

Kate gasped. How could she fail when her cousin needed her so? But be- fore she could speak the "Old Lady" chimed in, "You have your muslin and your blue sash— tie your curls with a riband to match and wear a rose. Do not be fright- ened. Carry your head high. Walk in forgetting they are strangers. Think of them as furniture." That made Kate laugh. What would

His Excellency think if he knew that his young hostess was regarding him as a two-legged table? And the smalt gallants clad in tight-fitting trousers as chairs.

She went to her room and dressed with great care. Tall for her age, graceful and slender, she carried her head well. Her clear hazel eyes were sparkling and intelligent. She had bright golden brown hair and a soft clear skin but her most at- tractive feature

A few bits of trivia:
Riband is a ribbon to match The King the men toasted to was King William IV born August 21, 1765 at Buckingham Palace, as- cended to the throne June 26, 1830 aged 64 years died June 20, 1837 at Windsor Castle. (Royal Family His- tory online 2015)
Londonderry Air a very old tune applied to Danny Boy lyrics by in 1912 by Frederic Edward Weatherly (1848-1929). It has an un- known folk music origin but would have been familiar to a Protestant family in the 1830s. Battle of the Prague written by Frantisek Kotzwara was a Czech viol- ist around 1757

was her wide generous mouth. She spoke to her reflection in the long pier glass; "No quaking nor shaking now" and went downstairs to the drawing-room.

When the Governor entered, she swept him such a graceful curtsy that everyone was charmed. Dinner was announced and at his request she took His Excellency's arm and sat next to him. The dinner went off well and happily. Mrs. Gray had trained a boy to wait at table and the decorations were much admired. Kate enjoyed it all, but slipped away before they drank the toast to His Majesty, King William. They soon joined her in the drawing-room for coffee and begged for a little music. A young lieutenant placed a tall beech wood armless chair before the satinwood piano which was one of the first semi-grand pianos to be imported to the colony. She tinkled out the *Londonderry Air* and after entreaties from the Governor added the *Battle of the Prague* which all young ladies were expected to know.

After playing for them and receiving the thanks and compliments of the guests Kate curtseyed and escaped. She flew to Mrs. Grey who was already feeling better and she amused her and the "Old Lady" by relating the compliments and drawing a picture of Lieutenant "Fatty" bringing her the tall, slender chair. She said, "I couldn't think of him as that kind of chair."

Early next day after thanks and compliments the survey party was off— His Excellency saying that he hoped to visit Eastbourne at a later date. The Major went with them but William stayed. He was rather intrigued and wanted to find a reason for Kate's very modest air and downcast eyes. He knew the Eastbourne family well and despite the fact that this pose was most becoming to her decided it must be regarded with deep suspicion. He could swear he had seen a gleam of mischief in her eyes when "Fatty" had rushed over with the piano chair. Mrs. Gray had been well enough that morning to re-arrange the chairs in the sitting-room and with Kate's help they seemed to be laughing with great enjoyment. What was the joke connected with chairs? Later on he found out how they had imagined each man in a chair or table. William said, 'Was I the bow-legged one?" And Kate replied demurely, "Don't forget that is the best rosewood, Mr. Talbot."

William

Then they began discussing his travels. He was to start them in the New Year, accompanied by a pleasant middle-aged tutor. He had made a solemn promise to his grandfather to do this and had been given introductions to European courts where he would see foreign customs and meet famous men and beautiful women. He would see life at its best and gayest, especially in Vienna and he would learn how important a place his own country held in the world. Then they talked of their old homes in Ireland. He told her that his parents

> This part of the story is about an Italian ring, Queen Elizabeth I her favoured courtier a young Irish girl in Van Diemen's Land, the passion of young love, brucellosis and heart breaking loss. The tale begins at the end.
> Read the full story in BOX FORTEEN: WILLIAM TALBOT, A RING AND CATHERINE

were dead, but he had an older brother lately married who hoped someday to bring his wife to visit him in V.D.L. He then described two rings given by Queen Elizabeth to his ancestors who had been her pages. These rings were called "Clodagh" and were handed down to each generation, for brides.

William's brother had given his to his wife and on William's eighteenth birthday his grandfather had given him the other asking him to make no use of it until after he had attained his majority and had returned from his Grand Tour. Kate asked "What is it like?" and he replied,

"You will see it one day Kate." He gave her a description of it— two very finely moulded gold hands, clasped over two large diamonds in a curious setting. At the wrist of each little hand is a gold frill, Tudor fashion, but what made the ring unusual is the tiny hidden spring under it which when touched causes the whole to split into five complete rings held together on one side by a tiny hinge. The two outer rings are plain the next two chased and the centre filigree. The workmanship is Italian, and the clasped hands typify "Love and marriage. "He said "I do not mean to take it with me because if I lost it, it would be irreplaceable. I must leave it here with my uncle until I return. Then looking earnestly at her he continued, "I shall be quite certain what I will do with it when I come back. Would you be interested if I write to your brother Humphrey or your father about my travels? We intend to see famous pictures and hear all the latest music." Kate smiled as she answered "I am sure we shall be most interested William." He must have gained some satisfaction from the brightness of her eyes because the anxiety in his relaxed.

Next day after thanks on both sides Kate and her escorts returned to Eastbourne much to the joy of the small girls. When leaving, William had asked Mrs. Grey if he might call again as there was only a month before he departed. She replied, "Or course we shall be very pleased to see you," so on one excuse or another with Humphrey or alone he contrived to call every day. It might be with a new book for the her father or with plants for Catherine's garden which she was trying to make as like as possible to the one they had left in Ireland. She planted tulips crocuses and sweet scented moss roses, mignonette, lavender, rosemary, pinks and laburnum.

One day he arrived with an invitation from his aunt. Would Mr and Mrs. Grey, Humphrey and Kate dine with them? An informal farewell dinner for William and his tutor. Most of their neighbours would be there. Fifteen was considered rather too young even in those days for a girl to attend a dinner and Mrs. Grey hesitated but her father noticing Kate's suddenly heightened colour said, "Now that Catherine has helped entertain His Excellency don't you think that further experience would be good for her my love?" Before Mrs. Grey could express any misgivings he had sat down at his desk and had written a note of acceptance and had given it to William. But Mr. Talbot was in no hurry. He had brought a list of roses for Kate and asked if he may assist her to lay out a border of primroses.

Putting on her Leghorn and taking a basket she said she would be glad of help and added that she must gather some flowers for the house. He immediately offered to go with her. They disappeared for quite an hour and were stunned when Lysbeth came running to ask Kate how many vases she would want. Lysbeth expressed surprise that the basket was still empty! William then recalled that his aunt had given him other notes to deliver so went to the house to say farewell after which Lysbeth remarked, "William is very happy about the party. He was sing- ing as he went down the trail. "Most of the surrounding settlers had been invited to the dinner. Some of their daughters were no older than Kate, so she felt happy. Her poise and her slim tall figure made her look older. The guests included the Legges, Parramores, O'Connors, the three Grey families, the Dumaresqs*, the Jennings and a Von Stieglitz who had arrived lately. They all knew one another so it was a happy gathering.

Kate wore an off-the-shoulder high-waisted frock. It was made of cream gauze with a wide cherry satin stripe and

*One of the guests at the party was Captain Edward Dumaresq (1802–1906) who arrived in Hobart in Oc- tober on the *Catherine Stewart Forbes* and was soon appointed Surveyor General and married Frances Blanche Legge, the youngest daughter of a Dublin barrister. He was granted land near Longford and named his property *Il- lawarra*. Like many other early pioneers his story is one of adventure and fasci- nation and is well worth exploring further.
Edward Dumaresq's Obitutary also makes for interesting reading

she wore a sash band hair ribbon to match, with a rose in her hair. She had no jewels for her mother thought them out of keeping with her youth. But she looked charming. William did not sit near Catherine. When arranging the guests his aunt had deputed him to take in a much older lady. Yet half way through the meal

Kate found him at her elbow, saying: "Miss Catherine I sent my man to ask might I have the pleasure of taking wine with you but you were busy with your neighbour. So I have come myself to beg the honour?" Kate blushed with pleasure. She knew of course of this custom of honouring a lady but she was too young to have experienced it herself. She felt now she was a woman of the world. How pleased Henny and Lysbeth would be when they heard of it! They would be sure to toast one another in tank water. While these thoughts flashed quickly through her mind William stood patiently waiting looking at her with his appealing eyes and charming smile prepared to touch her glass with his. She lifted hers. Conveying his to his lips he murmured, "Much happiness and good health", and to her startled ears added, "My little love." Confused, she hurriedly raised hers to her lips and responded,"A happy voyage and a safe return Mr. Talbot." He then bowed and returned to his seat.

When Mrs. Talbot gave the sig- nal, the ladies went to the drawing- room while the men settled down to toast

His Majesty, their wives and daugh- ters and William and his tutor. Meanwhile the ladies were enjoying themselves im- mensely. It was not of- ten they got together. While the men discussed

Home politics**, farming, the Govern- ment and the convict question, the women talked of news from Home, the lat- est fashions and reci- pes.

The girls gathered round Catherine. They had heard of her acting hostess for Mrs. Grey. They admired her for this, as- suring her they them- selves would have swooned with fear. Wasn't she nervous? And were any of the suite as interesting as the local beaux? In the candle light and the glow from a blazing fire the big room made a delightful picture. The gentlemen wore dark green or plum-coloured coats, ruffles and knee breeches with silk stock- ings and buckled shoes. The elder ladies wore turbans often feathered.

**Patriotic War Fund

Their English 'Home' was never too far from their hearts and when the call to arms for the Crimean War is carried across the oceans Patriots for Empire are only too willing to help, including those as far away as Avoca, Tasmania. Listed in the newspaper, in June 1855, were the names of contributors, the most gen- erous being Roderic O'Connor, £100, Simeon Lord and Humphrey Grey £20 each. Interestingly Humph- rey was accompanied by his Innes grandchildren, possibly Catherine, 11 and Elizabeth aged 9, to the meeting because their names ap- pear under his as donating ten shillings each.

Classified Advertising. (1855, June). The Courier (Hobart, Tas. :1840 – 1859), p3 Retrieved October 3, 2015, from http://nla.gov.au/nla.news-arti- cle2485801

Humphrey Grey...	...	20	0	0
Miss Innes	...	...	0	10	0
Miss E. Innes	...	...	0	10	0

Being after Waterloo they wore Empire dress with very short waists and de- cidedly low necks, with gauze scarves. The puffed sleeves were short and very full and the skirts long and made of rich striped silks. Reflected in the big wall mirrors were all these gay colours and with them scarlet high-necked uniforms. Many of the officers, including Lieutenant Champ (later to become the first Premier of Tas- mania) were stationed at the Avoca Barracks, a military post for the 68th Regiment.

One of the young sparks helped to entertain by singing in a melting voice —

Drink to me only with thine eyes at the same time rolling his at any lady near.

It was quite a feat to do this because of the high boned military collar. The girls tinkled on the pi- ano and there were a few more songs and choruses then a general move to say good- bye and to wish William bon voyage. A manservant carrying lanterns called the name of the owner of the barouche or gig as it came round and with the escorts on horseback quite a gay cavalcade went down the road. The ladies had wonderful cloaks and furs mostly, of seal or sable, which were bought to last a life time. Catherine's cloak, like that of the other young girls, was of cream cashmere. Hers was trimmed with a key pattern of narrow cherry coloured velvet and the cherry velvet hood made a charming frame for her small face.

> "Drink to Me Only With Thine Eyes" is an old English song and remains a popular song today with lyrics from Ben Jonson's 1616 poem "Song To Celia." Bliss Car- man, et al.,eds. The World's Best Poetry Volune II Love 1904. As a matter of interest a Sable is a marten with a short tail and dark brown fur native of Japan and Siberia and valued for its fur. Martes zibellina, family Mustelidae (Oxford Dictionaries Online – sighted August 12, 2015)

The night was bright but the roads not yet made. Part of their way was just a bush track where escaped desperate convicts might lurk or the traveller be stuck up by bushrangers or frightened by war-like Aborigines. Every man carried arms and had a loaded pistol in his hand.

Farewell

Two days later William paid his final visit to Eastbourne. Humphrey, Catherine's brother, who was in his confidence contrived that he should first see her father alone. Kate did not learn the purpose of this visit for two years.   He told her father that on his return he meant to settle on his own property. He then would ask permission to pay his addresses to Catherine for whom he felt an affection such that he knew neither time nor distance could lessen. He was quite sure that she was the love of his life and when he returned she would be old enough to decide. Might he write often to the two Humphreys and give them a full account of his travels, and would they tell her and keep her interest alive? I le was so carnest that Kate's father could only smile and give him his promise. Much relieved William went off to see Mrs. Grey and the girls.

He had wine and cake with them and then said good-bye rather more formally than usual.

He thanked Mrs. Grey for the hospitality she had always shown him and she replied that they would all miss him and would look forward to his return. He then asked had she no commission for him in Europe? Could he send her some lace from Malta or Brussels? He promised Lysbeth a clock from Switzerland and Henny a doll dressed a-la-mode from Paris. He paused then, and Henrietta with her usual impetuosity said, "But you will not forget Kate, will you William?" Kate in horror said, "Henrietta". But he answered "How could I? It was to be a surprise but now perhaps I should ask her would she like a little Italian arm-chair?"

Kate who had been rather pale and quiet became rosy and looked at him with sparkling eyes and said, "Nothing could be happier Mr. Talbot." She knew it would bring happy memories of the Governor's dinner and William's curiosity. He smiled, took Mrs. Grey's hand and, kissing it, murmured, "Your servant Ma'am." Then he went to Kate and doing the same, added, almost under his breath, "Always." He smiled charmingly at the small girls and was gone. They saw him for one moment as he halted at the turn of the road, took off his hat and waved it.

He wrote regularly to the two Humphreys, giving a full description of all he saw and did. They followed his journeyings on a map and looked forward to his return. In about two years Catherine had grown to be the belle of the district—her slenderness and pretty carriage were much admired and she was attracting more attention than her parents wished. This was inevitable when so many young settlers kept arriving but she had a gentle mischief equal to most occasions.

One day she was at Rockford talking to Miss Winston, the pretty young governess there, when they heard a horse cantering to the homestead. In a few minutes down came a breathless young man, a new settler who was building a very comfortable home on his grant. He bowed, facing Kate, took off his hat and addressed her, "Madam, they say that you and I are fated to go through life together. Will you not agree?" This was too much for Kate who barely knew him. She looked quickly at her companion and said, "I think Mr. N. is speaking to you Margaret."

She told the rest of the story to her mother. "He did not say another word. He struck his boot with his whip flung off to the stables, got his horse and went home! When we went inside to Mrs. Grey she said that never again would she receive Mr. N. because he went off without a word of farewell or apology. We said nothing and thought it best not to explain!"

About this time Catherine's Aunt Quain sent her a beautiful frock. She had seen it in a Dublin shop and could not resist buying it for one of her nieces. It was a creamy brocade, soft and richly embroidered with little green Irish harps. It seemed almost too handsome a dress for a young girl but the fashion then in vogue was simple. The bodice was closely-fitting, short tight sleeves, a rather narrow, deep square-cut neck, a high waist and very full skirt. The only trimming was lovely Limerick lace at the neck and sleeves. It hung so softly it would suit a tall girl admirably and was being kept for Catherine's eighteenth birthday.

She spent all her spare time in the garden. The flowers and plants William had given her were growing well and she wanted him to admire them. Meanwhile she would look hopefully along the track along which he would ride. No letters had come for two months but with the uncertain postal arrangements that was not surprising. He had not forgotten them. For Mrs. Grey came lovely lace from Brussels, Henrietta's clock from Switzerland, a curious pipe and snuff box for the two Humphreys and a very smart and exquisitely dressed doll for Henrietta.

While they were in Italy studying pictures and sculpture William had an opportunity of keeping his promise to Kate. There was great excitement at Eastbourne when a little round-backed Italian walnut armchair arrived. It was upholstered in soft floral tapestry. Kate was charmed beyond words. William had put in a note, "This is your laughing musical chair!" And when she sat on the arm from it strains of music.

But William was never to ride along that track again. At the time his ship was expected his uncle found he was not on board. A passenger brought a letter. He and his tutor were both at Naples, ill. They had Neapolitan fever (brucellosis). His grandfather and brother hurried post haste across Europe to get the best medical care for them. The tutor, older and tougher, fought his way to recovery but William, never strong had found it beyond him. The next boat brought news of his death and much sorrow to relations and friends.

Young Humphrey, knowing all about his feeling for Kate, was much upset. He said to his father, "Catherine, what can we tell her?" His father, greatly grieved, said, "We must tell her the truth." The poor man had to tell his young, tender-hearted daughter, who said nothing for a moment then very quietly, "Are you quite sure,

Papa?" He showed her the letters from William's brother and tutor in which they said that in his delirium William had said over and over again, "Not long now Catherine. I will not be long, my little love." Her father gave her the letters, kissed her gently and left her alone.

No one could comfort such sorrow. She must bear it alone but the rest made up their minds to make continual demands on her thoughts and time. She was an unselfish girl and must be made to feel how necessary she was to them. By the following boat a delayed letter came from William asking her father if, with Catherine's permission, they might announce their engagement as soon as he returned. If so would her father give her the enclosed letter? This was done, and she read:

My Dearest Little Love,

Ever since I left you, I have been longing to send you this letter. When you get it, you will know that your parents have given me their per- mission, with your consent, to announce our engagement. I cannot tell you how delighted I am, and how the days drag. I am counting them. My grandfather is anxious that we should see the famous pictures here and Naples will be our last port of call. Then I shall have the pleasure of telling you that neither the beauties of Spain, France, Norway nor any other country, can hold a candle to Miss Catherine Grey of Eastbourne. My uncle is keeping the old ring till my return, then, if you look along the track, you will see a man on horseback, galloping to bring it to you, my very dear, lovely Catherine. I wish

I had wings.

Your most devoted and loving servant,

WILLIAM

Not long after this letter the ring came. Her parents made no remark when she put it on her engagement finger and was never seen without it until the end of her life.

She was a beauty admired and loved for the sweetness of her disposition and later on owned a fine property in her own right but no man could persuade her, and several tried, to let him replace that ring.

Soon after the sad news, the little girls came home for their holidays. Their parents, to spare Kate, went to meet them at Avoca and told them about William. They were very distressed. Henrietta, always very fond of him, said, "He told us he would be our brother when he came back." Mrs. Grey explained that if he had re- turned

It would have been so and asked them not to say much to Kate, it might upset her, so they were very quiet. When they arrived at the house she was in the garden

7 Catherine Grey

so they ran to hug her but she was not their Kate, so thin and quiet with all the sparkle gone from her lovely, shadowed eyes.

That night she was tucking Henrietta in her bed when the loving little girl put both arms round her neck saying, "Dear Catherine, there is no one like you. You will always be the dearest one in the world to me!" She did not mention William but all the time she was at home she followed Kate like a puppy and would call her for any service, making Catherine feel how they needed her. In years to come, Henrietta and Lysbeth's children and grandchildren grew up to think, "There is no one like Aunt Kate!"

William's uncle had told everyone about the ring to spare Kate and he thought it right to make the intended engagement public. They were all very kind to her though their sympathy was unspoken. It took the form of asking her to join many riding parties or a game of croquet or anything to make variety.

Fortunately there was a continual coming and going of young settlers, although not all were of equal culture or good manners but it was good for Kate to meet them. She could help them and her parents and the small girls continued their demands on her thought and time. She gradually became the pivot of the family and when death made gaps and the marriages of her sisters drew them far apart, they clung to her. She was the means of keeping them together. Their children were sure of a welcome and warm- hearted understanding at her home. [vi]

William Talbot

Little is known about William except that he came from an ancient Irish aristocratic line- age whose estates and castle were Malahide near Dublin. His family had lived there since the Twelfth Century. A relation, the Hon William Talbot, had been given a large land grant at Break- o-Day and he named it Malahide after his home in Ireland. The property still exists today and owned by another branch of the family.

Malahide VDL

Malahide, Van Diemen's Land London : Royston & Brown

A Mr Talbot is recorded as arriving in VDL on Friday June 1st 1832 and there is an entry with Mr Talbot leaving for Sydney on November 29th 1833. These dates fit well with the family story but his relationship with the Hon William or indeed any of the Talbot family remains a mystery. It has always been accepted that the Hon William was his uncle but Stephen Talbot, the family historian can find no trace of young William and his place in their genealogy.

Humphrey, his father's right hand, was an unselfish, intelligent, affectionate boy. No one could be more loving or charming than he was to his mother and sisters. His first thought was to help his father succeed in this new life and so secure their future. With his happy infectious laugh and pleasant manner, no one in his company could be dull. He sang and whistled about the house and at work, though Catherine had seen him pause in his ploughing and look wistfully along the road when the Redcoats passed. Then he would determinedly shake his head, start whistling and ploughing again.

It had been no small sacrifice to give up his chosen career especially as he had listened to regimental tales from his childhood. But he could not let his father come to this new life alone. They were pitiably ignorant of farming, soil and the feeding and care of animals and very few books on agriculture were obtainable, so Humphrey took every opportunity of talking to experienced, practical farmers. It was late in life for his father to change his occupation and Humphrey knew he must try to gain all the knowledge available. It was not difficult to get assigned labour but a master must know how to direct it.

There were difficulties and disputes about boundaries. An unscrupulous neighbour altered the marks at night so that he could get more access to the rivers. If the Surveyor-General had enjoyed a settler's dinner rather too well he might wave his hand vaguely, "Here is your line Mr. So-and- So," and would ride away perhaps to a place nearby where the same procedure would occur, followed by disputes not always amiably settled. It was often necessary to go to the Head Office.

The Greys unfortunately had an unpleasant neighbour. They would have been quite ready to settle things happily but he threatened them with a law-suit if any of their animals strayed on his grounds. There was much clearing as well as fencing to be done and it was no wonder there was so much confusion.

At last Humphrey went to Hobart Town to consult Gellibrand, their family lawyer, and he wrote to Eastbourne, on June 3 1834

> Joseph Tice Gellibrand, (1792–1837) was the Attor- ney- General of Van Diemen's Land and eventually after con- flicts with Governor Arthur he became instrumental in the settlement at Port Phillip. He was killed in Victoria by either Aborigines or bushrangers af- ter being lost for some time in the wilderness. His full story is readily available. The two families were eventually to unite eighty years later with the marriage of Ethel Grey Dougharty and Laurence Ash- ton- Jones 17th June 1914. (Laurence was descended from Tice Gellibrand's family through his mother, Amy Christian Dixon)

:

My Dear Father,

I arrived in Hobart Town on Sunday, when I found that your new equipage had started the evening before. I have settled our business as far as Springs Corner.

Wedge had changed the line of Crook's Lane, but Frankland had disapproved of it, and had given orders to have it changed at once. The place where the sheep yard was, I will not get, as it appears it is about a chain inside an angle of Stephenson's Lot31.

Frankland would not change the way Wedge measured, as he said He said that I had no occasion to come down as he does not think that Lord would be foolish enough to go on with it as the damages he would get would be one farthing and not less than 40/- costs. He said it is one of the most trying cases he ever heard of. I am certain of getting Lot 31.

The weather has been very wet. Will you send Briggs to meet me? Come as far as Pages on Friday evening. Let him take his rations in a knapsack and a couple of feeds for the horse. He can leave the horse and return.

Major Lord's case is tried to-morrow. It excites great interest. Persons are coming from the country in great numbers to hear it.

It is almost certain he will be transported. Tell Margaret I will give her all the news when I see her.

I am, my dear Father, Y our affectionate son,

H. W. GREY.

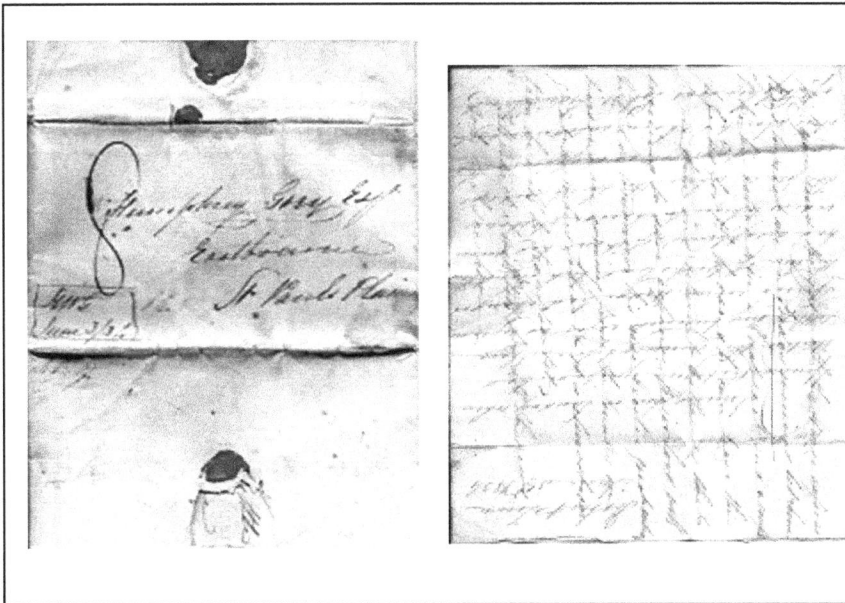

The orginal letter sent by Humphrey to his father

WRITER'S NOTE—

Wedge—Assistant Surveyor-General.

Frankland—After whom a Launceston Street was named, was the Surveyor-General.

Gellibrand—The lawyer, afterwards lost exploring Port Phillip. Mr. Simpson—A Hobart Town lawyer.

Every Grey was a born horseman. At four years old Humphrey would learn to ride a fat pony and he continued progressing until he could join the hunt.

At last their horses could be sent from Ireland to Van Diemen's Land. Amongst them was a young, unbroken half-wild beauty and Humphrey longed to school her.

He took a carrot or lump of sugar out to the paddock for several days and was so gentle and persuasive that at last she allowed him to slip on to her back. She trembled but his hand was soothing and all would have been well but for the foolish prank of a wretched boy who had come to watch and give unwanted advice. He did what he regretted to the end of his days. He suddenly banged a tin at her heels and in her terror she bolted, kicked and threw Humphrey violently into the bole of a large gum tree and he was killed instantly. Nothing could be done and they carried him into a heartbroken family. Young Humphrey was buried in the private family burial ground on Rockford, where two or three young cousins were soon to lay along side. It was a strange thing, that though they loved horses and rode so well yet more than one met his death through them. Basil, Major William's eldest son, died on a Victorian hunting field and the same thing happened to a young nephew, yet Basil's youngest brother hunted in all weather, still he was over eighty.

Mrs. Grey roused herself from her deep grief to thoughts of her husband who adored her. Never very robust, small, frail and lovely, she had borne without complaint, separation from the family and friends with whom she had grown up, but the long and tiring journey and the settling into a new home in such strange surroundings, had naturally undermined her health.

> Humphrey was not the family's only loss. Sa- rah Anne Grey was Baptised at Mallow Parish, Cork, Ireland on the October 1810 and presumably died young. Source: Irish Births and Baptisms

Family Cemetery now on Benham

Figure 17 Gray Private Cemetery with Rockford in back- ground. by Annie Rushton 2016

The Gray family cemetery is located two kilometers along Royal George Road from Avoca, on the left had side traveling East. Humphrey Grey may, infact, have been the first to be buried at the cemetery. People believed to have been buried here include:

Humphrey Grey 30 January 1836.

Anne Gray 25th April 1837 aged 77. Mother of William and James

James Vincent Grey jnr, drowned on his birthday in 1838, aged 10. Son to James and Mary.

His grave stone remains

Ellen Gray, baby to James and Mary. Born 1 Feb 1839 and died soon after of General Debility on 18th March 1839

Richard Gray 28th November 1839, aged 16 drowned at Chain (Marsh) Lagoon. Son of Wil- liam and Ellen Gray.

Dora Kingsley, died Nov 1844, aged 11. Died of fever. Daughter of Samuel Bell Kingsley and Dorethea. Samuel was Mary Gray's brother. Her grave stone remains.

Other people who were possibly buried here although at this stage families may have been obliged to use public cemeteries;

William Gray died on 10th March 1848. James Gray died on 18th May 1849

Unbridled Loss

Humphrey Grey died from horrific injuries on 30th Jan 1836 as a result of a riding accident.

James and William's mother, Mrs Anne Gray (nee Kingsley) died on 25th April 1837 aged 77 and was presumably buried at the Rockford cemetery.[vii]

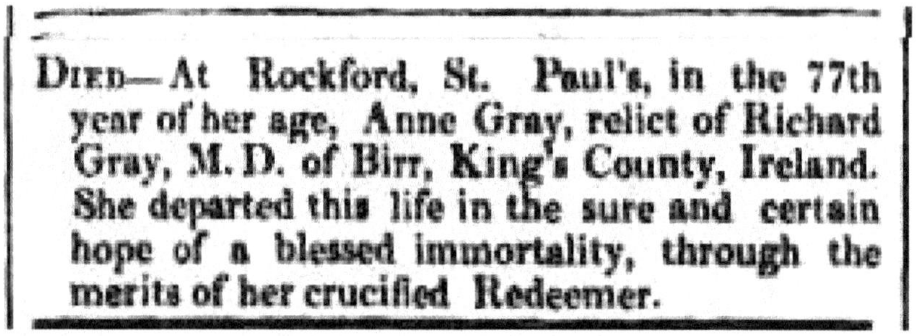

DIED— At Rockford, St. Paul's, in the 77th year of her age, Anne Gray, relict of Richard Gray, M. D. of Birr, King's County, Ireland. She departed this life in the sure and certain hope of a blessed immortality, through the merits of her crucified Redeemer.

The following year James and Mary were to lose their son through drowning. On the 15th November James Vincent was crossing the St Paul's River when the cart he was on turned over, killing him. He died on his tenth birthday.

Within a few months the couple were again to experience the loss of a child, their seventh. This time a baby, Ellen born on1st February 1839 and died of *General Debility* six weeks later on18[th] March 1839.

William and Ellen were not immune from the heartbreak which had so cruelly affected the other families. Their son, Richard also drowned 28 Nov 1839 aged 16 but at a place called the Chain (Marsh) Lagoon.[viii]

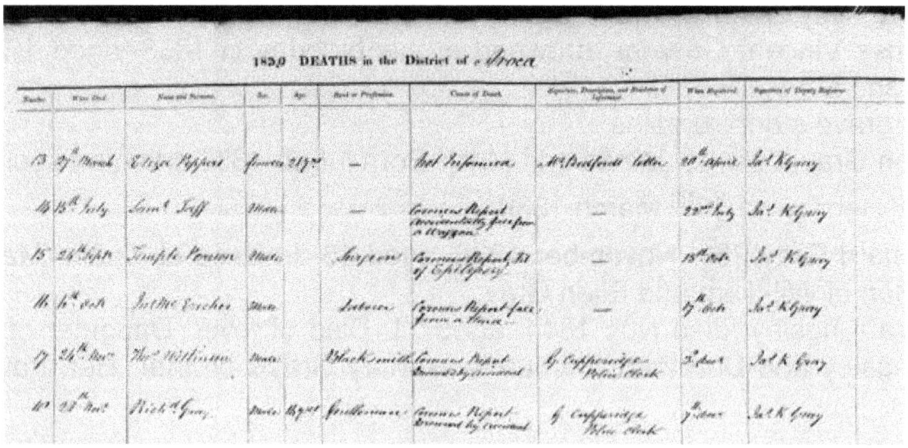

Figure 24 1839 Deaths in the District of Avoca. Rich'd Gray Male 16 years Gentleman

Finally a poignant note recorded from afar by a Missionary Rev. Nathaniel Turner;

"By sunrise next morning he left for Avoca and Paul's Plains, nearly fifty miles distant, Mr. Gleadow kindly driving him halfway. In the afternoon, in company with the Rev. W. Butters, of Ross, he visited Major Gray and family. It was somewhat remarkable that in that neighbourhood three related families of the same name, "Grey," had lately suffered bereavement by the sudden death of the eldest son. Two of the young men had been drowned.

The other had been killed by a horse bolting, and dashing his rider's head against a tree. The visit, which was one of condolence, was kindly received."
Rev Nathaniel Turner 1839

Carrying On

Fears for her precious children should they run into Aborigines, bushrangers or snakes filled Mrs. Grey's mind with daily tremors. She loved hospitality and was

a wonderful little house- keeper and had many friends. For the sake of her husband and girls, she made a val- iant attempt to carry on, yet Humphrey's death shortened her life. The small girls were still at school and the house seemed so empty. Catherine became accustomed to doing any secretarial work for her father.

She would ride over the place with him and her journal really helped him. She entered all events and transactions in it throughout the years and perhaps that was why her memory always remained so clear.

She not only recorded social events, but the names and wages of all house and farm workers and the dates on which they came and went. As the years went on her father depended more and more on her. She was such a help and comfort and when for the last few years of his life, he lost his sight, she was there for him to depend on.

One great wish she and her father and cousins shared. There was no church at Avoca, and they were anxious to build one. Their names are in the first of the church records as Founders of the Church which was named St. Thomas. They bought some land in a high position overlooking the "Meeting of the Waters." It took some years to complete the church and the beautiful avenue leading to it. In it is the highest pulpit in Tasmania. Under it sat the clerk striking his fork and determined to keep the congregation in tune.

> ### Avoca Church[x]
> St Thomas' Anglican Church (Romanesque Revival style), designed by James Blackburn, who also Designed the church at Port Arthur. Consecrated on May 1842. Three wealthy men, Mr Simeon Lord, Humphrey Grey and Major William Gray, stood as guarantors for the cost of the building. Some of the pews still carry their original numbers and at the back of the church is a large pew built for a particularly large church warden Avoca Museum Information Center David Masters. Read more in Volume Two

On the pulpit itself was a very large hour-glass to keep the rector's eloquence in check and each cedar pew had entrance door. The church was not finished when the girls married so Dr. Bedford officiated in the home for both occasions. There were a few outstanding social events in which Kate and her father took part. One was a ball in 1837 for Sir John and Lady Franklin, given by the Bachelors of the Northern Division of the Island. The invitation was on a small, embossed card, on the back of which were the names of the members of the committee. The secretary was N. Connolly and the Bachelors were: John Sinclair, J. A. Youl, J. Cox, J. R. Kenworthy, Rich- ard Dry, J. H. Wedge and W. Mann. The invitation read:

"The pleasure of Miss Grey's company is requested on Wednesday evening the 15th inst. at a Ball and Supper to be given by the Bachelors of the Northern Division of the Island in honour of His Excellency, the Lieutenant- Governor and Lady Franklin. Launceston—February 9th, 1837. An answer is requested."

Later on an invitation was sent to Kate and her father for a dinner party at the Cornwall Hotel given by Sir William and Lady Denison who were visiting the North. At that they met the most prominent and interesting personalities of the day.

Figure 18 Avoca Church Prout, John Skinner, 1805-1876.

Henrietta and John Thompson

Humphrey 1880 - 4th May 1868
= Catherine Mahony 1779 - 5th Nov
1847 of Mallow, Co Cork on Feb 1806

Henrietta Emily 1820 - 28th June =
Thompson 1819 - 12 June 1899

Henrietta Emily	Alexander John d 18 April 1875	Catherine Isabella d 19th Oct 1927	Lavington Grey MD d 24th Oct 1923	Florence Margaret d 16 April 1879	Elizabeth Alice = Captain John Mackay of Inlochberrie, Scot-land in 1887	Ada Grey died aged 23 years

				Alexander Dudley b 1888 = Mabel Adams or Norman	Major John Shaw MD b 1890 d 20 Nov 1934	Ronald Grey b 1891	Kenneth Scott b 1893 Died in action 1915

Figure 19 Image by Richard Chuck

Henrietta

At eleven years old, in 1831, Henrietta was already a wise little woman with the biggest of black-lashed blue eyes, fine straight brown hair which grew in plaits to her waist, a lovely skin and an aquiline nose. Her curved mouth hadn't the gaiety of little Lysbeth.[xi]

The elder girls taught their younger sisters to read and recite and also to play little tunes on the harpsichord but their parents wished them to go to school as the elder ones had done. They watched the papers eagerly, hoping to hear of a suitable school for Henrietta, where she could have a wider curriculum to study.

At last, in that year, an advertisement appeared— "Mrs. Clark, of Ellenthorpe Hall, Ross, a cultured gentlewoman, is prepared to take a limited number of boarders. These would be instructed in every branch of female education. French, astronomy, the use of the globe, needlework of all varieties, plain and fancy, painting, music and dancing, for the moderate fee of £90 per annum. Every attention would be paid to deportment and they would be practised in the usages of polite society". The advertisement added that on a certain date two bullock drays would attend Avoca for intending pupils from the surrounding districts.

On making enquiries the Greys received such satisfactory reports that they decided to send Henrietta. Several of her young friends were going too. The drays with mattresses, cushions, rugs and one or two low chairs were comfortable. A

Like all families there were constant changes as children grew through different phases of life. By 1831 Henrietta was old enough to go to boarding school. This was also a practical move to place her away from the dangers of their situation and the fact that they did not have a proper house to live in. She was sent to Ellenthorpe Hall run by a delightfully eccentric woman Mrs George Clark, formally Hannah Maria Davice, in their home just outside Ross. Feared dangers however were to follow the children.

Read more about the school in Volume Two

sensible, pleasant chaperone of the advanced age of thirty and some armed, middle-aged escorts on horseback accompanied them.

The girls with sandalwood boxes of clothes and a large plum cake each met the drays at Avoca and began their long journey at the usual rate of three miles per hour. The bullockees were far too restrained in their language to hurry them. But it was all fun for the girls. Their escorts gave them a sense of security when they had the thrill of meeting poor Aborigines wandering from place to place, looking for a resting-place in the land which was once their own. Or they might meet families of new settlers like themselves travelling in drays or rather wild- looking men on rough horses, who went past hastily as if anxious to escape notice and the girls whispered anxiously to one another, "Bushrangers?"

Figure 8 Ellenthorpe Hall near Ross / H.G. Lloyd Allport Library and Museum of Fine Arts

9 Figure 20 Thomas Dodd, 'Ross Bridge', undated

The escorts too would look grim with their pistols ready but nothing happened. En-route the girls spent the night with settlers they knew whose own girls might join them. It was carefully planned. Hospitality was warm and sincere and no one thought of refusing it. Their host and hostess enjoyed hearing the news. Mrs. Clark was as good as her word. She had a roomy house and a large, well-kept garden, brick-walled. Everything was well run and as they were under the protection of the nearby barracks, what could be safer? The girls were taken for pretty country walks and watched making of the beautiful bridge[xii] planned by a gifted convict architect and worked by the chain gang.

10 A shakoe Illustration by Richard Chuck

The convicts later gained their freedom for doing it so well. The sight of them in their dreadful clothes did not upset the girls. They were accustomed to assigned labour, Henrietta's family though had brought out house workers with them. Once a month Mr. Clark called on the officers at the bar-racks and invited them to spend an evening at the school. Then the older girls would take it in turn to act as hostess. All the carefully inculcated rules of etiquette must be observed. Mrs. Clark appeared as their chaperone only. Next day if criticism were warranted she made it! There were to be no "wall flowers" if they danced. They made their own orchestra. Girls must curtsy gracefully. Programmes were arranged beforehand and carefully printed by the girls themselves. The girls prepared all food and drinks. They did not always dance. Sometimes they had a musical evening and to that each girl had to contribute something, with the result that they learnt to forget themselves and to think of others' enjoyment. It was a pretty sight to see them smiling, blushing and after a time quite at their ease when they danced with the young bloods who enjoyed this break in the monotony of their daily drill and came polished to the hilt. It was thrilling for the girls to see a regiment on the march. The men's shakoes* showed over the top of the school wall and how could it be helped if intriguing little notes blew over the top?

When Lysbeth joined Henrietta a few years later one little note written to Lysbeth caused the girls great joy when it fell at her feet:

Dear Miss Elizabeth,
I have often longed to gain permission to call upon you in your own home and to further our acquaintance, but it is, perhaps, better not. I feel a nearer approach might dispel the pleasing illusion.
Your unacknowledged admirer.

11 Henrietta courtesy of QVMA

In her later years Mrs. Clark would laugh when asked if she deliberately sowed the seeds of romance by buying her house in such a position? Henrietta was with Mrs. Clark for about seven years. Because of transport difficulties, she only went home twice a year and after three years she brought Elizabeth with her. It was a great happiness for all when they came back to Eastbourne. The house lit up. There were riding parties and a lot to hear and tell.

Henrietta at eighteen was very companionable when she left school, but Kate had her at home for a few years only. Henrietta soon married her old friend John Thompson** whom she met again at a friend's house. He was delighted to see again the little girl who mothered her dolls so well on the *Mary Ann*. Now she was a charming, poised, though still small girl and she completely bowled John over. He asked if he might call and was graciously given permission. The result was that in a few months they became engaged and were married the following year.

*For those unfamiliar with fashion of the 1830s the following may be of some assistance. A Shako is a stiff military hat with a high crown and plume. (Merriam-Webster online dictionary) A brocade is a rich fabric woven with a raised pattern, typically with gold or silver thread (*Oxford Dictionaries* sighted March 2015) while Indian muslin is a lightweight cotton cloth in a plain weave (*Ox- ford Dictionaries* sighted March 2015)

Her father liked John and there was no reason for delay. He was well off and could give Henrietta every comfort. Her father gave her a farm. Since Humphrey's death Mr Grey saw no purpose in holding so much land.

There was a tenant on Henrietta's farm and proved very useful to them later on.

12 Henrietta's Marriage Record – Tasmanian Archives

At her wedding Henrietta did not wear white but like Lysbeth, who had married before her, her frock was blue-grey taffeta. It was called 'French grey' and was much in vogue then. The tiny, high waisted, off-the-shoulder bodice was criss-crossed with pleats. Hen- rietta's dress was so small that years later no girl of fifteen could squeeze into it but vanity must suffer pain even if it meant lacing tightly on one's wedding day.

**The narrative about John Thompson is confusing and reads as though he and Henrietta had met as children on the *Mary Ann* but this does not appear to be the case. The Brig the family came on was the *Ann* in 1829 and John arrived some years later to Sydney as an adult in 1843. His life story does however make for interesting reading which is presented in some detail in his obituary on June 14th 1899 in the *Launceston Examiner. (Tas:1842 - 1899)*,
p. 5. Retrieved September 27, 2016, from http://nla.gov.au/nla.news-article39807624

Portrait of John Thompson, c 1840, attributed to Thomas Bock. Image In- formation: QVM **Registration No:QVM:1991:P:0003**

On their curls they wore lovely Limerick lace which fell in a cape over their bare shoulders and down their backs in a little train. Kate as bridesmaid looked beautiful in soft blue, rose patterned brocade.

In later years when Lysbeth's children came to stay at Eastbourne, Henrietta's were brought to play with them. The latter were always clad in the most delicate, hand- embroidered Indian muslins, Leghorn bonnets and pretty white fur coats for warmth. The little cousins, Lysbeth's children, in their plain, sensible, Holland frocks, bound with Turkey red, were almost too overcome to pull them about in a game of hide-and- seek which they all loved. But through Aunt Kate's tact and kindness, they were all one family and when, later in life, their fortunes were reversed, they always remained friendly.

There was nothing denied Henrietta's children, yet the elder boy, Lavington grew so fast and was so thin that doctors suggested a long sea trip and he was sent off to Edinburgh to finish his education and later to do a medical course.

When first married John loved to entertain and give rather lavish dinner parties so he and Henrietta engaged a large staff of servants. It was almost too much for Henrietta who was accustomed to a much quieter home life. It tired her but John, who enjoyed showing hospitality was happy. Henrietta preferred the quiet of country life and fifteen years, later through a complete change in their circumstances, she was to have it.

Changing Fortune

Firstly two of John's ships laden with cargo were lost at sea and secondly, a man in his firm absconded with a large sum of their capital and John found himself bordering on bankruptcy. He talked it over with his wife who said the only thing to be done was to dismiss the staff, sell the big house and all unnecessary contents and take the family to her farm which happened to be vacant.

John felt this deeply but agreed. He hated to take Henrietta to the small, rough house after the big airy one. There would be no one to cook or care for the children. Henrietta would have everything to do and he had meant her life to be all roses. Yet with her practical common sense Henrietta made the best of things. John was no farmer but he toiled early and late on the farm. The younger son learned to milk but they could not quite make ends meet. Henrietta almost wrote to her father but knew that an appeal to him would hurt John's pride. The children were only getting the education that she had time to give them and that grieved the parents very much.

This went on for two years. It was almost Christmas time when Catherine and her father suddenly appeared in a comfortable barouche. They had had no idea of the state of affairs. Though Catherine and Henrietta corresponded nothing had been said of John's losses. Knowing her love for country life Catherine had taken it for granted that John's money had made the farm a pleasant place for Henrietta and her children. But now they noticed broken fences, poor animals. Everything seemed to shout poverty. They were appalled.

Even the children were shabby. Still they were all bright-eyed and healthy. Plucky little Henrietta was very thin but said not a word about their change of fortune. John always courteous welcomed them and the children were delighted to see them. Henrietta said they would have tea but had nothing to offer them but home-made bread and butter. It caused great excitement when Kate produced a big cake baked for them by Mattie who had remembered their taste. Also there was a large box labelled, "Not to be opened till Christmas Day." Kate asked them all to come to Eastbourne and share Christmas with their grandfather.

While the children settled on the cake like a swarm of bees the elders talked and read a long letter from Lavington in Edinburgh. They were determined that he should know nothing of their troubles and be able to finish his course. When he had left home his father had placed sufficient money in an Edinburgh bank for this purpose. Kate noticed the brightness of their eyes as the letter was read. Lav. was doing well and that raised their spirits. The Greys returned home to Eastbourne and next day Kate raided her bottom drawer and every sandal-wood chest. She was determined to send Henrietta all the help she could. Her father sent a cheque for £200 and a note—

My Dear Little Daughter,

You and John have not forgotten you have a father, have you? It is a long time since he has given you a Christmas box. He wants to make up for that now and John must not deny him the pleasure, so-let me hear that you have spent it on something that each of you can enjoy.

The tide is sure to turn for two such brave people. Hoping you will have Christmas with us.

Your always loving father, HUMPHREY GREY.

The gifts soon arrived and little Henrietta wept with joy. So did John but only the birds knew. His feelings were mixed. While grateful for the gifts he could not bear to think that anyone but himself should bring relief. He had always been generous and when his ships had plied between India and Australia he had ordered and got for Henrietta and her sisters the most lovely heavily-fringed, embroidered shawls and thick, creamy silk, also embroideries of all sorts, the finest muslin handkerchiefs and such like.

But while he ploughed, his brain worked. Now his old firm had been obliged to close down and he did not mean to continue on the farm so he had to plan a new outlet. His friends and he had a good many were working for him too so shortly after Christmas he was able to bring his family near to town, as he had received an appointment as secretary for the Mutual Fire Insurance Company and several other directorships.

They had a comfortable home again and at least a cook: The children went to school. Alec went off to the Grammar School. He was anxious to do law and being bright got through his university course quite early. He was then articled to a well- known firm of solicitors, but there trouble came. He worked with a young man who developed T.B. and he contracted the disease too, fatal in those days. Alec was a gay, charming lad of 22 then. He wrote such happy letters to his cousin showing his enjoyment of life. In one, he wrote,

"Have you heard the latest news of H— M—? Talk of going from Scylla to Charybdis!* He was paying too much attention to his mother's housemaid, so she packed him off to an aunt* in Bendigo, but we shortly heard that her housemaid's charms had quite over- come him, and he married that one!

"We have had a brilliant Aurora Australis lately. It had been an undisguised blessing!

Now when one calls on a beauteous maiden, it is quite "comme il faute" to invite her, with "mamma," to take a stroll in the garden and exert one's brain to discuss the beauty of the Aurora. Shortly Mamma will find that the warmth of the fireside appeals to her more than the wonders of the sky and she will leave you to entertain her fair daughter !"

Alec soon became too ill to continue his work. It was usual then to keep T.B. suf- ferers from every breeze, shutting up doors and windows and Alec's two lovely young sisters, Margaret and Ada, who contracted it as well, both died from it in their early twenties. Everything possible known then was done but it was of no avail. John heard Henrietta cry, "O God, you are so great. What

have I done that you should take my children?" It tore his heart, she had been such a wonderful little mother.

Both John and Henrietta lived to be old— John was eighty when he got pneu- monia. Dr. Lav. returned from Scotland and knowing their life-long devotion to one another was afraid for his mother who had a weak heart. He persuaded her to lie down for a rest, but she had hardly left them when they had to tell her that all was over. She came back into the room and kissed her husband on the forehead mur- muring, "I will not be long, John." A few days later she kept her word, dying in her sleep on the

28th June 1899.

One happiness they had had. Their youngest daughter, Elizabeth had mar- ried John Mackay and brought her little sons, Alexander,   John, Ronald and Kenneth from Queensland to see them.

*The term 'Being be- tween Scylla and Charybdis' is an idiom deriving from Greek mythology, meaning "having to choose between two evils". Several other idi- oms, such as "on the horns of a dilemma", "between the devil and the deep blue sea", and "between a rock and a hard place" express the same meaning (Wikipedia). Also *"comme il faute"* refers to being correct in be- haviour or etiquette (Oxford Dictionaries March 2015

14 Sarah Elizabeth (Lysbeth) Innes (nee Grey)

13 Believed to be Elizabeth's wedding dress

Elizabeth

Lysbeth, as they called her, was the youngest of the four Grey sisters. With a rose leaf complexion,* she was small and fair. The others had dark lashes and brows but to her sorrow hers were as fair as her hair. Her eyes however were darkly blue with such warmth and kindness in their expression that with the gaiety of her lovable, impetuous nature, they drew everyone to her. She had friends everywhere because she was so friendly. She also had a soft, infectious laugh in which everyone unconsciously joined. In her company

*A 'Rose Leaf Complexion' is basically when someone has fair skin and pinky red cheeks

no one could be dull. At the age of seventeen she went to stay with the Giblins, relations of Dan's in Hobart. Here she met a young Scotsman, Frederick Maitland Innes, who, loving adventure, had come to V.D.L. with the intention of settling here. At the age of eighteen he had run away from the lovely Scottish home of his guardian-uncle to fight in Spain. His father Captain Francis Innes, fought under Wellington and died of war wounds before Frederick was born, in 1816.

His uncle arranged Frederick to be sent home and for two years managed to keep him fairly content. They had a mutual love of literature and the library was well stocked. The uncle planned a professional life for Frederick but the young man thought the idea much too dull. He was determined to see the world and especially the New World so he and his school friend James Scott, both clever young men, went off to conquer it and did later help to make Tasmanian history. Frederick was twenty-one and Lysbeth seventeen when they were married in 1838 at Eastbourne by Dr. Bedford.[xiii] Frederick was by way of being a dandy. He wore a dark, cut away, tailed, cloth coat and striped peg- top trousers, a silk stock and a light blue waistcoat, with very pretty gold and blue enamel buttons. He wore fine black and white hand-knitted silk socks and buckled shoes. His fine grey eyes shone with admiration when he saw his bride and she was equally satisfied with his appearance for, though not handsome, he had fine features and hands and according to the fashion of the day wore side whiskers.

In Lysbeth's trousseau were the daintiest little lace trimmed caps to tie under her chin at night to keep her curls in order, while her husband had soft, woven, tasselled night-caps!

Lysbeth's father did not wish her to marry so early though many girls did but after their losses he could not bear to deny his girls anything they had set their hearts on so he agreed to the marriage, settling on her a small property, Mona Vale, in the neighbourhood and stipulating that they should make their home there. So they did for a few months then Lysbeth returned to her father, for Frederick, summoned by his mother, had to return unexpectedly to England.

His mother had

Frederick had arrived on the Brig *Derwent* on the 4th February 1837 and certainly matched Sarah's intellect and insight. Their relationship bloomed over the next year and they were married on 13th July 1838.

> At East Bourne, St. Paul's Plains, on the 31st ultimo, by special license, by the Rev. William Bedford, junior, Frederick Maitland Innes, Esq., (Editor of *The Colonial Times,*) fourth son of Capt. Francis Innes, late of her Majesty's 10th Regiment of Foot, to Sarah Elizabeth, third daughter of H. Grey, Esq.

Frederick led a long and distinguished career in jour- nalism and then politics. He held strong convictions and beliefs including being secretary of the Aboriginal Protec- tion Society in England, he was an anti-transportationist, supported free trade and was a Presbyterian lay leader. In politics he became a member of the Lower House, the Upper House and became Premier of Tasmania in 1872.

---

not heard yet of his marriage and being very frail wanted him to return at once. He showed the letter to Lysbeth and her father and they agreed that he should go if a berth could be got on a good ship which was leaving next day. The two young things felt the separation very keenly but at Eastbourne her father and sister were secretly delighted to have Lysbeth until Frederick could find a suitable home in England. Meanwhile she treasured

Frederick's books and he sent her the latest Dickens and Thackeray which they all enjoyed. Frederick's mother rallied when her son arrived but was so frail that it was some months before he was able to leave her to take up literary work and find comfortable lodgings in London for Lysbeth and himself.

In England

After Frederick left V.D.L. the Greys immediately wrote to cousins in Ireland and England and as quickly as possible warm-hearted replies came back to them. Sir Richard Quain, famous London surgeon and   John, his brother, who had rooms in the Inner Temple promised to do all they could for the young couple. This set Humphrey's mind at rest.

Later, a very charming letter written by John Quain to his mother, who sent it on to Eastbourne, gave them great pleasure.

Soon though Lysbeth was to leave for Scotland to be with Frederick. Sailing ships really only had two choices for their trip 'Home'. The trade winds in the Southern Ocean were perfect for the outward voyage but were unassailable for the other direction. So ships either chose to go north and around Australia, sometimes to Mauritius and then below South Africa and north again to Europe. The alternative was to catch the trade winds, below New Zealand, through the Drake Passage, Cape Horn and then north some- times to St Helena and on again in a north easterly direction across the Atlantic to England.

Elizabeth describes it thus;

A voyage of about two months duration from the Australian shores bought us within the welcome sight of the first land which relieved the blue monotony of our prospect, on the morning of April 8th 1841. Going upon dusk, at about a quarter past six o'clock, I saw an immense rock, which with the deception common to objects at sea, appeared close to us in a north – easterly direction. This was St Helena, a spot familiar to my imagination & my thoughts from its connection with perhaps the most wonderful mortal who has trodden our earth. The Island presented a bare, rugged, aspect. The only indications of verdure in occasional vallies, which came under our notice in the vessels track to a safe anchorage. James' Town, the capital of St Helena, is situated in one of these vallies, & is encompassed by precipitous hills: vessels anchor close to it in the only situation from which the town can be seen at any distance. There were several there at this time, whalers, and a Queens brig employed on the African coast on the look-out for slavers.

The complete letter makes fascinating reading and brilliantly scripted and may be found in Appendix B

Dated 1841.

My Dear Mother,

You have already heard of the arrival in London; of Elizabeth Grey, or should I say Innes.

I was not a little surprised when I returned home on Saturday, and after I had written to you, to find on my table a letter from Catherine with a card in it inscribed, "Mr. and Mrs. Innes". I took the earliest opportunity of calling on Elizabeth, and you will be pleased to hear that I spent the whole of yesterday, Sunday, with her and her husband. I cannot tell you how pleased I was with her.

I need not say how delighted she was to see some person in so strange a place as London, that she could call her friend, and introduce him to her husband.

But really, I think she is a person with whom anyone would be taken with, even at first sight. She is somewhat what I remember Margaret to have been, at her age. Of middle size, light hair, approaching almost to sandy, smart, pretty figure, intelligent countenance, very pleasing, affectionate, in short, Irish manner coupled with an agreeable, lively, but shrewd method of expressing herself, which is taking in the extreme.

I have been thus minute and particular in her personal description, of which I know you will be anxious to hear. You may all be better able to form an opinion for yourselves, of one, whom I am sure you will be delighted to see.

She arrived on Tuesday, but I suppose you have heard of her journey, as she has written to Alice.

Just imagine what an undertaking for so young a person to travel half around the world, alone, without a friend or protector, but those she happened to make on her journey, yet she went through it all in such good spirits and at the same time, with such excellent tact that she made the whole journey pleasant to herself and so short that she says it seems only yester- day that she parted from her father. She is very, very anxious to see you all, but particularly Uncle, of whom she speaks just as her mother would.

Alice's and my letter reached V.D.L. only four days before she sailed and she says the receipt of my letter, knowing that I should be in London, was the means of relieving her father of much of his anxiety on her behalf. I am so glad therefore, that I am so fortunate as to be here. I have devoted so much of my space to speaking of Elizabeth that I have not yet said a word of her husband. But, I assure you, it is not easy to stop praising her. I feel that I could go on for ages on such topics! If you just consider her extreme youth and the distance she has come, alone and unprotected to her husband for whom her affection is unbounded, the sufferings she underwent on his account, which you must hear depicted in her own language, and then remember it is two years since she left the Colony. You must bear all this in mind and then see her, you will admit that it is enough, without any family feeling, to stir up all the latent romance in a person much less excitable than myself. But now a few words about Mr. Innes.

He is a young Scotsman, but without any of that harshness which is apt to repel in the Scottish character. I like him much. He is, indeed, a very superior young man. His tastes, which are literary, unfit him for Colonial life. He is a man of much reading and very extensive information, indeed a person whose acquaintance I should have been   glad to make under any circumstances. I have delayed writing to John (a cousin) until I have conversed with Innes about the Colony. He says if John really has a taste farming, it is

So Lysbeth and her husband were warmly welcomed by all the relations. In later years, when their son, aged 12 was sent to join the Royal Navy at Dart- mouth College, twelve thousand miles away from home, Richard and Lady Fanny, his wife, and John showed him the greatest kindness. There were quite a number of Grey and Innes relations to befriend the boy.

Two of the Innes sons were born before the family returned to V.D.L. Humphrey Grey was born in London and Frederick Maitland, in the Isle of Wight, where Frederick introduced Lysbeth   to his mother's relations.

The return to V.D.L. took a wearisome six months. Lysbeth had no nurse and was always anxious about her babies. Rats were a menace on board ship. Still much to the joy of her family Lysbeth Frederick and the boys arrived safe and sound.[xiv]There was so much to hear and tell, though it was amazing how much the prolific, criss-crossed letters had already told them. Emily Grey was a particu- larly fine correspondent. No detail escaped her and she kept her Uncle Humphrey in touch with the ever moving army of nephews and nieces and could always be relied upon to give the latest news and where the regiments were stationed. One of her letters arrived before Lysbeth.

Dated 1840.

My dearest Uncle Humphrey,

I could not think of allowing an opportunity to pass, without sending you a few lines (they were 12 crisscross pages) by Mr. Henry Prim. I hope this will find you, my aunt and cousins in the possession of perfect health and happiness.

I also send you a prayer book, which my dear lamented father read with attention, made it his constant study and derived much benefit and comfort from. My mother wrote you a long letter, in which she mentions Basil's visit to Ireland. We were very happy to see him after so long an absence. I suppose Mamma told you of the death of Major Reke, to whom Eliza, Basil's sister was married. Basil mentioned that she intended coming over from Ireland. She has two children, a boy and a girl and with her own and their pensions, will have four hundred a year, enough to give them a respectable education. (She then launched on a full description of her sister Gertrude's children).

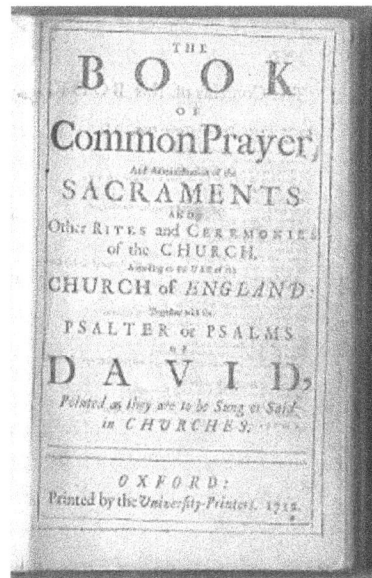

Gertrude's eldest, Eliza, is now twelve years of age. She has an interesting and intelligent countenance, dark hair and beautiful dark eyes, her figure is slight and graceful.

Olympia is a fine little girl, with a countenance of good humour and animation, brown eyes and hair, the colour of my dear father's. Her complexion is fair and blooming. She is more like her mother than her father.

Jane (another sister) has three fine boys. The eldest is five years old. We think he is like our dear departed brother, Basil William — the same bright blue eyes, fair skin and sweet smile.

I had a long and most affectionate letter from Humphrey dated 1838. He is expecting to get his Lieutenancy soon. He does not think that the 9th Regiment will return to England for seven years. He is a very good correspondent.

Basil told us that the 45th will shortly be ordered to Upper Canada. French is appointed assistant collector of customs at St. Pedro. Caroline and her husband (Lieut. Smythe) are at Trincomalia. She has two sons. My aunt Ursula still resides at Jaffa, and is in excellent health.

My dear mother, I am happy to inform you, is quite well. She and I and Jane and her family, all went to Kingston for the summer, and there met aunt Sophia (Uncle William's widow). She is an extremely good-natured per- son, and is very well provided for, having, in addition to her pension, the allowance left by Colonel Drouily, for the widows of officers, who died in con- sequence of wounds, received in the Peninsular War. Besides that, she owns a good property in Queen's County. Later:

Humphrey has received his Lieutenancy in the 39th Regiment, Madras. Basil's sister, Sarah, married Dr. Russel, and on their way home from India on leave, their ship was wrecked. She, her husband and servants were all drowned. They left two fine boys, who their uncle will now bring up.[xix] Uncle Warburton with his Regiment, the 56th, has now left for Jamaica.

Basil is a great favourite with us all. Such a fine, well informed young man. He has just been promoted to a company in the 75th Regiment, on account of his brave defence of Newport, against an attack of the Chartists. He is now at Windsor. You could write there to Captain Basil Grey.

Do you often see Mrs. Creery? Please give her my love. She mentioned, in her letter to her mother, how very kind and attentive you and yours have been to her. She likes V.D.L. I often send you a Kilkenny Paper, as I am sure you will like to hear how poor old Ireland is getting on.

Pray have the goodness to write me a long letter. Believe me, dearest uncle, we are most anxious to hear from you. I shall be on the lookout for a letter from you or from one of the family.

Mary and Nancy are faithful servants. They are both alive and well and beg you will accept their good wishes for the happiness of you and yours. Mary has lived forty years with my mother and Nancy nearly as long, soyou can imagine how attached we are to them, and I think they are to us. They felt and participated in all our troubles and trials and are deservedly loved by us.

I am sure you are tired of reading this wretchedly written letter, but it is written in much haste with a bad pen. But I have heard that Mr. Henry Prim, who is taking it, leaves in three days. Friday, 14th February, 1840—at 10 p.m. Our young Queen was married, last Monday, at 12 o'clock to Prince Albert.

Kilkenny was very brilliantly illuminated that evening in honour of the happy event. The town really looked extremely gay. How beautiful London and Dublin must have appeared that night! I should have liked to have a peep at the splendour and. brilliancy of London that evening.

Believe me, with Best Wishes and Love to you and ours, Your sincere friend and affectionate Niece,

Emily Grey.

Adieu! may God Bless you! Write me a long letter immediately on receipt of this. Don't forget to send me a newspaper often.

Meeting Relations

Not only did Lysbeth meet her own relations again but Frederick took her to see his mother, his elder brothers and sisters, and she heard a great deal of their family history. This she was able to tell her children later and they, as time went on, corresponded with their overseas cousins and kept in touch with them.

One young grand-daughter [Katie Dougharty] with Catherine, her mother, wrote their history beginning with the account of her great grand- father, Francis Innes, Frederick's father who, like the Greys, had been in the Regulars

The couple left the Isle of Wight ten days after Frederick was born and endured a very trying voyage back to Hobart on the *Mandarin*.

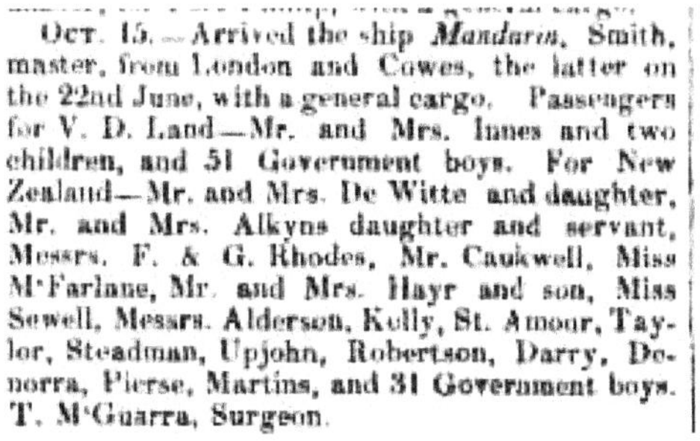

Oct. 15. — Arrived the ship *Mandarin*, Smith, master, from London and Cowes, the latter on the 22nd June, with a general cargo. Passengers for V. D. Land—Mr. and Mrs. Innes and two children, and 51 Government boys. For New Zealand—Mr. and Mrs. De Witte and daughter, Mr. and Mrs. Alkyns daughter and servant, Messrs. F. & G. Rhodes, Mr. Caukwell, Miss M'Farlane, Mr. and Mrs. Hayr and son, Miss Sewell, Messrs. Alderson, Kelly, St. Amour, Taylor, Steadman, Upjohn, Robertson, Darry, Denorra, Pierse, Martins, and 31 Government boys. T. M'Guarra, Surgeon.

Figure 36 Oct 15 – Arrived the ship Mandarin, Smith Master, from London and Cowes with a general cargo. Passengers for V. D. Land – Mr and Mrs Innes and two children and 51 Government Boys Reference xv

This was partly due to the fact that Frederick was acting as superintendent of Parkhurst boys on the voyage. These were juveniles from the age of 12 to 15 who were rehabilitated at Parkhurst Prison on the Isle of Wight and sent to Australia and New Zealand with the aim to apprentice them to local settlers. Elizabeth detailed the birth of each of her children in her Bible; Complete list in Appendix B: Grey Family Tree

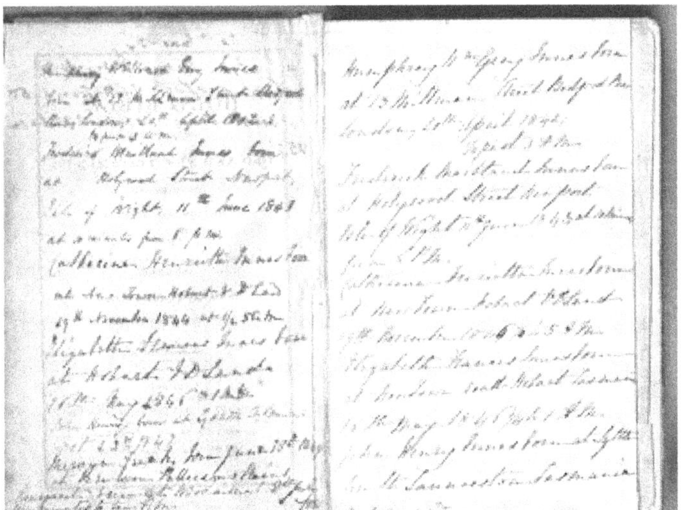

Written by Kate Hamilton Dougharty

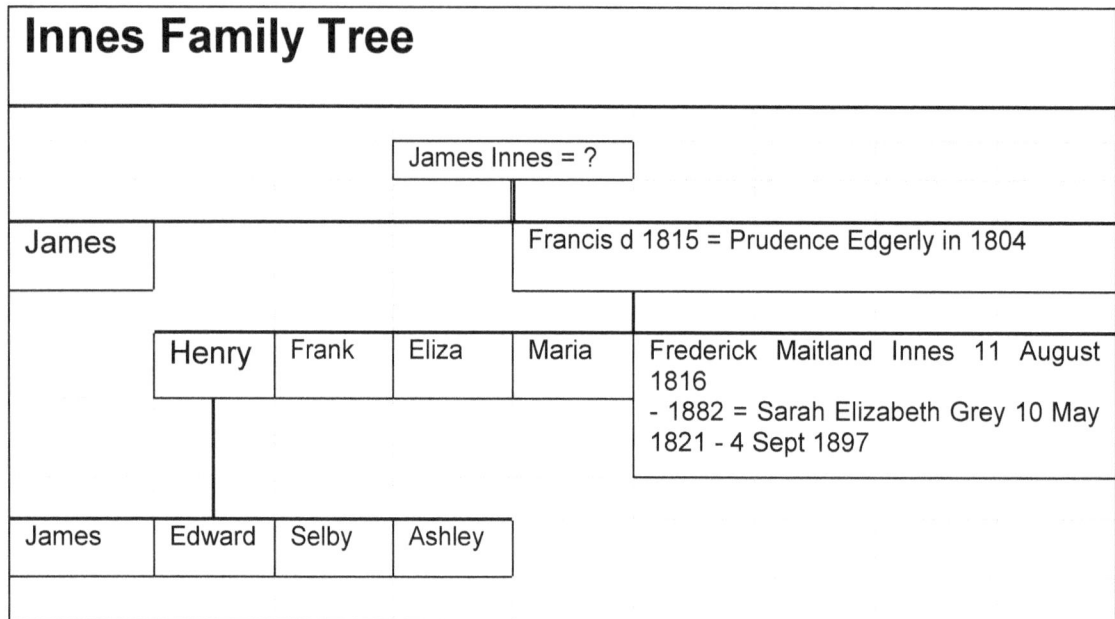

Innes Family Tree

	James Innes = ?			
James		Francis d 1815 = Prudence Edgerly in 1804		
	Henry	Frank	Eliza	Maria	Frederick Maitland Innes 11 August 1816 - 1882 = Sarah Elizabeth Grey 10 May 1821 - 4 Sept 1897
James	Edward	Selby	Ashley	

FRANCIS INNES

In 1804 young Ensign Francis Innes from Scotland was stationed with his Regiment, the 10th, on the Isle of Wight awaiting orders from the Duke of Welling-ton now engaged in pursuing the elusive Napoleon. Meanwhile Francis was keeping himself and his men in the highest imaginable state of drill and polish. Woe betide the luckless 'Tommy'* who dared to appear before him with a button missing or with mud on his spotless Wellingtons! He had no intention of allowing Ensign Foster's men to outdo his. So his company shone from head to foot.

*'Tommy' is a term used for a sailor and 'baccy' for tobacco. Pantalettes are long underpants with a frill at the bottom of each leg, worn by women and girls in the 19th Century,

He had blue eyes, brown smiling cheeks and snow white teeth. His scarlet coat, high boned collar, white waist-coat and stock, lightly powdered hair, tightly fitting red-slashed trousers and high shining boots made him a very presentable young man indeed! At 11 a.m. one fine day he left the Barracks to reconnoitre the village street with the cosy thatched cottages and the lovely church on the hill overlooking them. The legend ran that the evil one had actually taken it to the foot of the hill one night but had been routed by the good spirit who triumphantly transferred it to the top of the hill and it had remained there ever since.

By eleven all men were at work and very few women were to be seen. The children were at school so the whole place seemed very sleepy and Francis was thinking of returning to Barracks when he saw a sight to behold. Coming towards him was the daintiest little figure in sprigged muslin. Noting the smallness of the sandaled foot below it he knew this was no healthy village maiden and his interest was stirred. She carried a basket, went in and out of the cottages and was fare-welled by an ancient man or woman. Francis pretended to be studying the contents of the shop window. Time was slipping by and he was due at the Bar- racks within a quarter of an hour. She appeared to be particularly interested in a garden but as she smiled at an old parishioner Francis managed to catch a glimpse under her poke bonnet and saw golden curls, round pink cheeks and the dark-lashed hazel eyes of Prudence Edgerley, the Rector's niece.

He vowed inwardly that he had to find out who she was. Years later Prudence confessed to her daughter that she'd hoped he would! Of course she had taken in at one glance the interesting scarlet clad figure. Next Sunday, having minutely inspected his shining troop, Ensign Innes marched them off to church noting with satisfaction that Foster's men did not look a patch on his!

Suddenly he lost his studied calm. Along the aisle rather hurriedly came the Rector's comfortable wife holding firmly the hand her seven-year-old twin boys, who were named Charles and Dick. To Francis' delight the other twin was also being steered resolutely by the lovely little cottage visitor rather pink with the struggle of getting there in time. The Ensign in his joy dropped his prayer book and did not pick it up. Including the sermon the service went on for two hours with nothing to sustain the old parishioners but their snuff or peppermints (wrapped in clean handkerchiefs).

Not only Prudence but the twins in spite of their mischief had faces of angelic sweetness. They had to sit one on each side of her but they took every opportunity to wink at or pinch one another behind her slim waist. Soon the length of the sermon lulled them to sleep, each with his confiding head on his mother's or Prue's shoulder. The dress of the period made such pictures of the boys — short, blue, brass-buttoned jackets, white frilled shirts, white pantaloons and square buckled shoes. And the twins had such golden curls.

The soldiers stood till the congregation and the Rector's family had left the church. During the sermon the Ensign's mind had wandered round in circles. How could he introduce himself? Then he became most relieved. In front he saw Mrs. de Lancey, wife of a brother officer Egad. Surely she would help him! Just as Prue passed him walking demurely down the aisle a little lacy, lightly scented handkerchief floated to his feet! Was it accident or design? He never moved so fast. He almost pounced and in a flash the handkerchief was transferred to his gauntlet cuff. Not quickly enough however to deceive the eyes of Private Jim Barnes who winked at Sam Brown who in the same way conveyed to his next in line the intelligence that the Lieutenant was smitten and about to make a sortie. But when the Ensign strode out and flashed a glance along their wooden faces no one indicated they had noticed anything. They filed out in perfect order into the pleasant sunshine where the villagers were being greeted by the Rector and his family and were gathered in groups for a gossip. Here the Ensign called on his men to halt then went straight to Prue saluting holding out the handkerchief and saying, "I wonder if this belongs to you? I picked it up." Knowing perfectly well that it did the minx looked at it thoughtfully, prolonging the moment for meet- ing the very blue eyes of the handsome young soldier and answered hesitantly, "It may be mine, or it may be Mamma's," and, turning to her Aunt said, "Is this yours, Mamma? The officer found it?"

Mamma having known young days, also looked at it carefully. "Why, I believe it is! How thoughtful of you to bring it, Ensign—?" pausing to give him a chance to supply his name which he did at once. "Oh," she went on, "I think Mrs. de Lancey has spoken of you. You come from Scotland, do you not? You must come to the Rectory and have a talk with my husband. He has lately returned from Scotland and would be delighted to see you. When can you come?"

Francis was beaming and Prue looking very demure when he said, "It would be a great pleasure. May I call tomorrow?" Then he was startled by a sudden sharp cough behind him (Jim Barnes had developed one. Then Francis went on, "I must return to the Barracks now, but, I shall come tomorrow, thank you." With heightened colour he bowed, saluted, and then in a severe tone ordered his men to march and as stiffly as a poker went grandly down the street. After mess he went to his room and wrote to his mother in Scotland expatiating on the beauty of the Island (not of its girls.)

Next day he called on the Rector and his ladies and made friends with the twins who thought him a good chap but wanted to know why he had not joined the Senior Service. From then on during the month that the Regiment was stationed in the Isle Francis would in his spare time turn up at the Rectory or was seen by the villagers carrying Prue's basket of delicacies to the sick ones. He came almost well known to them all and his friendly smile and manner were quite approved of by them.

Pranks

On one of these walks Prue told Francis a story about the twins. They were attending the village school but were soon to go to boarding school to prepare for entering the Royal Navy at the age of twelve, determined to be Nel- son over again. They had heard all about the battle of the Nile in 1799. Trafalgar had not yet been fought. The only time they were known to be still or serious was when an old salt came to the Rectory and told them all he could of ships and Nelson. Yet through their idol they fell from grace.

One morning the Rector was having a constitutional up the village street when it seemed to him there was more bustle than usual. People staring over their gates, looked very serious. He was just about to ask the reason when to his aston- ished gaze there appeared two miniature Nelsons. Each had a black- patched eye, an arm in a sling, a wooden dirk on his hip, carrying a cane and had on a three cornered paper cap. They were followed by two small Jack-tars, pig-tailed accord- ing to fashion and apparently chewing tobacco which they spat out noisily as they walked with rolling gait.

Horrified, the Rector thought surely no one would dare poke fun at Nelson? Then he recognised his own small sons! Giving a swish of his cane and followed by scandal- ised villagers he drove them into school. Here in the sternest voice they had ever heard he bade them strip off their slings, patches and dirks, saying, "How dare you show disrespect to the man, who with the help of God and our ships, is saving our country from the enemy! How could you do such a thing! I am ashamed of you!" Then he turned to the school master and said, "They must be punished. Caned severely to make them think!"

The twins, very white, had not said a word in their own defence, but then Charles cried, "But Father, we do have respect" and Richard went on, "We wanted to be like him in every way. We think he is wonderful,

Figure 23 Illustration by Richard Chuck

Please!" Their serious faces made the Rector believe them but he could not allow even an apparent want of respect in front of the villagers so he said, "I want you

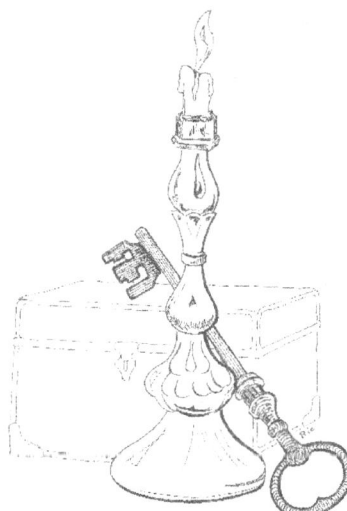

all to look up to Admiral Nelson, who has given his eye and his arm to save this dear country of ours.

He could stay at home now but nothing will content his brave spirit until he is sure Boney [Napoleon] cannot come here. Let us give three cheers for him," which they did, with a will, and the Rector went home.

But Charles and Dick stood straight to face ε   ,
"Please, you do know we did not mean it? We thi   ϶
world." Dick went on, "We were not making fun of him. We wanted to be exactly like him," and then they held out little, scratched hands and the school master gave each brave hand five quick light cuts with the cane. The poor man was not enjoying himself at all.

Then the Jack-tars, Ben and Sam, ran forward holding out two dirty little paws, crying, "Us too. Us was the tars as follered them!" But he thrust them to one side and left the hall. Sam later said to his parents, "He was that white, I could swear 'e was blubbing," and his father replied, "You be careful, my lad, or I will see that you do!"

But the incident made a great impression on the village. Next Sunday the Rector had his largest congregation. The villagers remembered the epidemic which had swept through the village ten years back when the Rector and his wife had given every ounce of their strength to help the sick. Both their elder sons, who were helping too, had caught the fatal germ of Spanish influenza and when Prue, who had been sent away, returned it was to a silent, sad house. Three years later the twins were born and from the moment of their arrival Prue adored them. She was an orphan who looked on her uncle and aunt as parents. Though often exasperated by the twins' mischief the villagers adored them too. They were such friendly little fellows. When the Rector saw signs of original sin, he would deal with it, but always remembering the older brothers with a pang in his heart.

.On this Sunday the twins sat up straight, resisted their usual nap and listened to the long sermon. It was on Nelson's watchword "Duty." They heard of the improvements and reforms he had made in the Navy. They intended never to forget and this village was later known as one that the press- gang need never visit. There were young men there always ready to man Nelson's ships. No matter now how much the twins were tempted they would no longer take part in orchard raids which had been fun, but they were not losers. Many a rosy apple was kept for the Rector's youngsters.

By the end of the three weeks that the Regiment spent on the Island, Francis and Prudence felt they knew one another quite well enough to know that life would be impossible if they were separated! Prue had met and liked Mrs. de Lancey and Mrs. Rossi, whose husbands were Francis' superior officers. She knew they followed their men. Why should not she and Francis marry so that she could go with him? But first, his mother must be consulted and there they met with a flat refusal. In reply to Francis his eldest brother wrote on behalf of their mother:

My dear Francis,
Your mother and I, on receiving your letter, were greatly shocked. We can- not give our consent, though we have no doubt that the young lady, whom you wish to make our daughter-in-law, is as charming as you say. But you are both very young, and you are asking her to share a life which we know to be

*The letter to Francis poses some confusion. According to research conducted Francis' father had died well before 1804 in 1789 and it appears to have been written by his eldest brother James on behalf of their mother.

both difficult and dangerous. You must remember too, that you are unable to give her the comfort to which she has been accustomed.

Your pay is not sufficient, and as you are my youngest son, I am unable to supplement it, except in a very small way.

We beg you to consider everything carefully. It would be most unwise to marry until you gain promotion.

Your mother and I are sorry to disappoint you, my dear son, but do be patient.

Your affectionate father, James Innes.*

When Prudence, accompanied by Francis, went to ask her uncle the reply was the same. Though very sympathetic and sorry the Rector and his wife could not agree to their only, most precious niece marrying a "Marching" soldier and not only face discomfort, but danger. Francis must gain promotion and be in a better position to care for her and Prudence, only seventeen, must wait his return. Prue said, "Mrs. Rossi and Mrs. de Lancey are going with their husbands!" "But," her aunt said, "So much older and more experienced, my love. Their husbands are seniors and would be provided with better quarters. No, it would be most unwise. Do not think of it!" The Rector, most distressed to see how white his beloved young niece had become, appealed to Francis. "If I could help you I would, but I am unable to make Prudence an allowance. The boys and their education must be our chief thought now."

Francis could say nothing. How could he expect them to make an allowance and sacrifice the boys' future? There was only a week left before the Regiment must embark for overseas. The villagers were much stirred. They had grown accustomed to awakening to the sound of drums and bugle calls and seeing the redcoats go by or in and out of their homes on lawful or unlawful business. The village girls would be disconsolate when they left. The Rector had already been asked to call the banns for some couples which would allow their wives be on the strength to go overseas with the army. In any case she could pack her man's kit and see to his mending and other little comforts. The twins were also very busy. Somehow or other they hoodwinked the sentries, slipped into the barracks, to see and report on all the preparations. All this went to Prue's heart. How could she remain behind?

Four days before they left, the neighbouring gentry and the villagers combined to give a farewell Assembly to the Regiment. It was a delightful sight, gay frocks and red coats mingling in graceful movements. They danced as their fore- fathers had done in country squares. The prettiest there was Prue herself in pale blue brocade patterned with tiny roses. The dress was high-waisted, very full, low-necked and short-sleeved and just reached her slender, blue ribboned ankles, and silver sandals. In her hair was a blue ribbon with one pink rose, and she wore black mittens. Her curls just touched Ensign Innes red-clad shoulder and over his high-boned collar and lace ruffles he bent his head and felt he could not bear it.

Leave Prue behind! He told her that his military duty would take him to the other end of the Island next day but he would be back at night. White and tight-lipped he said, "Prue, my dearest little love, I know I should not ask you to face hardship and danger. I should not! And no home to offer you but a cottage in a rough village. Nothing you are accustomed to! How could I ask so much? Your guardians are wise to refuse, but Prue it is terrible to leave you! It may be years before I can return! What can we do? A special licence can be got and used in three days, but it is wrong to persuade you!"

The Elopement

There was silence for a few moments, then Prue looked at the imploring eyes above her and said quietly, "It is no use, Francis, they will not change their minds. Get the licence to-morrow. I will be ready. I will not let you go alone. Other girls go with their husbands. Papa married Mattie (the twins' former nurse) to Jim Barnes to-day. Why should we be different?" So it was settled.

Francis got the licence and the night before the Regiment left, a little after midnight, he rode to the Rectory with a rope ladder fastened to his saddle and a dark cloak over his bright uniform. All day Prue had been pale and quiet although she had been helping in all rectory activities. Being an orphan for years she had lived with her uncle calling them Papa and Mamma. That day her aunt, saying nothing, looked at her with concern and sent her out with the twins who were bothered too. What had happened to their dear, gay, adoring sister? Was she fretting because her friend, Ensign Innes, was leaving for the war?

He was a jolly nice chap. Knew quite a lot about fishing and had a brother in the Royal Navy and could tell them a little about Nelson. But he was always turning up. That was a nuisance! When he left for overseas, they would get their devoted slave back again.

Poor Prue! She did feel shaken that night when she tucked them up in bed. They hugged her so warmly. She and their parents, a little tired from the excitement in the village, went to bed early. She was undressed when her aunt came into her room to kiss her good-night. But she was soon dressed again in a warm, soft, blue merino frock, her blue fur-lined cloak and bonnet and boots, so that Francis would find her ready. There was still over an hour to wait. She packed a few small necessities in a bag and sat down, to write to both parents, hoping that might give them a little pleasure. Then she put on her warm gloves, blew out her candle and waited at the open window.

When Francis had placed his ladder he climbed up and lifted her down very carefully with her bag and muff and put her on his horse. Then he jumped on too, shook the reins and they were off! Drowsily, the Rector and his wife registered the galloping but little dreamed that their hitherto docile niece was eloping with her handsome young soldier or that miles away a sleepy old cleric was being roused from his dreams to marry them. He was shown a special licence and was asked to perform a war wedding ceremony. It was quite in order and not unusual at that period. So in the quiet dullness of the lovely old Carisbrooke church with no witnesses but the verger and his wife the two most concerned were soon made happy. Who could separate them now?

XV

The Vicar who was a locum tenens and had not met Prue

15 St Mary's Church Carisbrooke illustrated by Frederick Hamilton Jackson

before, shook them warmly by the hand and wished them all happiness. Francis, who was responsible for duties at the barracks, took Prue to her old nurse in her village home but the latter was so shocked she begged them to go to the Rectory and explain.

They went. Prue woke her guardians and broke the news, who were naturally a little hurt but realising that the deed was done set to work to make the best of it. Before he left for the barracks Francis looked at the Rector with such honesty in his beautiful eyes as he said, "Believe me, sir, I do realise what a wonderful thing Prue has done, trusting me, and I mean to spend the rest of my life putting her happiness first!" And the Rector believed him. Francis kept his word. For the ten years they spent together his one thought, apart from his duty was to care for her.

There was no time to get any new clothes for Prue so her Aunt looked through everything that she had to try to augment the things in the little bag. To her surprise she met an almost unbreakable will in her small niece and that, in Prue's future life, was to stand her and her children in good stead. The Rector insisted on giving her a few guineas he had in the house and even, much to Prue's grief—for she knew what sacrifice it meant-drew out for her all his little bank reserve. The next day her uncle and aunt, the twins and all the village went down to the sea to watch the embarkation. Fortunately it was a lovely day. Against the blue sky, the fully rigged troop ship, lying off shore, all sails unfurled and flags flying, looked most beautiful.

There were farewells from old men and women who knew they might never see their sons again but there was no outcry nor lack of self-control. Boatload after boatload of young, straight-backed Redcoats went off to board the ship. Prue, Mattie and all wives were already there. When all were aboard the bugles and drums sounded. The long row of soldiers was reflected in the clear water, a vigorous sound of cheering reached the group on the shore and received a fainter, but courageous, response from these. Then the great ship turned slowly, headed into the breeze and towards Spain.

The twins shouted and did their best to help. Holding tightly to their parents' hands they did their utmost not to cry. They had lost their dear, precious Prue! They could not have imagined that someday in future Prue's sons and grand- sons were to serve under them. With a few friendly words to the villagers the Rector and his wife went home, not talking much. It was quite an hour later that the twins went into Prue's room and found the letters she had written.

My Dear, Dear Uncle,

Please do not mind very much, I must go with Francis, but not without telling you that I shall never forget the love and care you have given me all   my life and I shall never, never be thankful enough to you. Francis feels the same and we are looking forward to telling you so one   day.

Your truly most loving niece, PRUDENCE.
Then there was the even-more-difficult one to write to her Aunt:

My Darling, Darling Mamma,
All day long it has been so dreadful, knowing that I was deceiving you all. But, please do understand—Francis is going into such danger and it might be years before he could come for me. If I am with him, he will have some happiness, so I want to be like the wives of other soldiers. I know we are young, but every day makes us older! He will be sure to get promotion more quickly if I am with him and

before we know it, the Duke [of Wellington], will be sure to notice what a fine soldier he is and how keen on his duty.

Please tell the dear twins that I love you all so much, it hurts dreadfully to leave you all, but Francis needs me even more. My heart will always be   full of love and thankfulness to you, my very dear.

Francis joins me in much love, PRUE.

Mrs. de Lancey and Mrs. Rossi, experienced travelers, showed Prue where her cabin was and Mattie came to help her to unpack. It was a great comfort that she was there. The sea journey to Spain did not take long but travelling over the cobbled road by mule-cart or horse was very rough and trying. Prue's friends did all they could for her—anxiety about their husbands kept them together and made them all very brave and uncomplaining.

War

A little over a year after they were married Francis came back from the battleground with the ever present sound of firing and roar of guns, tired out and sad from the terrible sights he had seen. He was greeted at the door of his cottage by a smiling Mattie who said, "The Mistress wants you sir". Francis was welcomed not only by his wife, but by the sight of their first child Henry. A future Captain in the Royal Navy whose children and grandchildren would themselves become sailors, one, in 1918, to be an admiral of the fleet.

As the years slipped by Henry acquired brothers and sisters; Frank born in Malta (where for years the women wore black hoods in grief that Napoleon, later driven out by the British, had conquered them), Eliza and Maria in France and last of all Frederick Maitland, born on Scottish soil. There had been several opportunities for Prue to go home but she would not without Francis. Battles were more frequent, Waterloo had not yet been fought and no man, unless badly wounded, could be spared. The children were healthy and though she longed to take them to her land, she waited.

As the campaign went on they were constantly moving and if stationary long enough wives would hide their growing anxiety, don their loveliest frocks and make their husbands forget for just a few hours the horrors of war. They would dance, but at any time might be interrupted by the sound of drums and bugle calls. Their partners, in their beautiful scarlet and gold, so soon to be soiled or stained, would bid them a hasty farewell and leap on to horses, brought by soldier servants and gallop to their stations.

Khaki had not yet been heard of. Highlanders, in their gay tartans, blowing their bagpipes struck terror into the hearts of the Frenchies, but the brightly coloured uniforms could be seen a long way off and so were dangerous for the soldiers.

The day that brought Florence Nightingale to waken the world's conscience to care for our fighting men had not yet dawned. So when husbands left for the field the wives went home, changed into simple gowns and from their cupboards brought out basins, bandages, clean rags, brandy or any simple remedy they could think of and always kept for emergencies. They knew that even if their husbands returned untouched there would be long lines of poor men, wounded and limping or rattling home in rough carts over the cobbles. There might be only a rough pavement for a poor men to lie on but if they were unable to lift him to shelter they could give him a drink to revive him and a blanket to rest on while they tried to bandage the wound, from which they shrank. They often felt inclined to faint but pulled them-selves together and did their best.

Perhaps sitting on the kerb to hold a poor boy's bandaged head, write down his name and any message he wished to send home would comfort him and the men, wonderfully unselfish always anxious about their mates were pathetically grateful. Prudence most anxiously would always look for men from her own Is- land. Unfor-tunately quite a number had been lost and there were of course no cables or telegrams nor even stamps so any news must be sent by soldiers invalided home. Prue wrote long crisscrossed finely written letters to the Rector with every detail of news she could gather so that he might tell his people. She never forgot her family and would talk to her children about the charming, winding streets, cosy cottages, gay gardens and beautiful churches of her beloved Isle.

By 1815 Prudence had been married ten years. She had carried her head high through so many trials and difficulties and now at last there seemed some hope of peace. Francis had gained his captaincy some time before and had been prom-ised further promotion. He was to be in command of a British possession in the Mediterranean and knew the Governor's residence there would at least be a com-fortable and pleasant home for Prudence and the children. Mattie was always with them. She had no children and Jim, her poor husband, had lost his left arm in battle not long before. He had gone through the ordeal of having most of his arm removed without chloroform. That merciful medium was not known until later. He was very weak, still unable to stand the journey back to the Isle and Prue was helping Mattie in every way to build up his strength. At present he was to stay with them.

Francis was to go ahead and see that all was well for transplanting the family who were to follow almost at once. He looked so happy and handsome as he kissed them all goodbye, saying to Prue, "It won't be long now, my little love, before you are the Colonel's Lady, "and getting on his horse, waved gaily to them all and was gone.

With Mattie's help Prudence began her packing. One evening the children were in bed and she was sitting by the fire in her parlour reading over the list of necessities that she must take when without being announced, Mrs. Maitland, the wife of Francis' C.0., walked in. Usually straight and smiling she was now so bent and white-faced that Prue ran to her saying, "Dear Mrs. Maitland, you are ill. Come and sit down." But the older woman stood and looked at her with mute agony in her eyes. Prue gazed then whispered, "Not Francis," and Mrs. Maitland answered, "Your husband and mine, too." Prue put her arm around her as she asked, "Are they—?" And poor Mrs. Maitland explained "Both killed in action—a courier has just come from Lord Hill to tell us." *

Prue said nothing. She saw again Francis' happy, gay smile as he promised that she should soon be The Colonel's Lady and talked to the children of their new, pretty home. So she sat down, dazed and stunned. Poor Mrs. Maitland was shaking. It had been a great effort to come to tell Prudence. It was only a year since her eldest son had been killed in action and now his father.

Suddenly Prue noticed this and with her lifelong habit of thinking of others took Mrs. Maitland's arm, saying, "You must sit down" and then pulled the long fireside bell- rope quickly and Mattie came in response. She looked at their white faces in horror and went out for biscuits and wine. She poured out and took a glass to Mrs. Maitland and then to Prue who mechanically took it but made no attempt to drink. Kind Mattie held it to her lips then saying, "Take it, Miss Prue, you must," and without consciousness of what she was doing, Prue drank, but could not speak.

Mattie, a little bewildered, asked Mrs. Maitland, "Is it the Captain?" and got a nod in reply, then looking old and broken the latter said, "I must go to my little girls."

Prue rose blindly remembering what an effort the older woman had made for her and said, "I will come with you." It was only a block down the street, so, in silence, the two poor things went, passing wounded, bandaged men and horses on the way.

Tragedy for Prudence

On Prue's return, Mattie, with baby Eliza, not yet two in her arms, came to meet her and took her to the fire, placing on her lap the tiny child who pressed loving little cheeks against her, calling, "Mamma." Mattie, who like everyone who knew Francis, loved and respected the Captain and was heart-broken. She could hardly bear to tell Jim who, until he was wounded, had always been with the "Captain."

Francis Innes, Captain in the 10th Foot of the Regular British Army, fought under the Duke of Wellington in the Peninsula War. As a young Ensign with his Regiment in the Isle of Wight, he fell in love, there, with Prudence Edgerley, niece of a local vicar and they eloped and were married in the church at Carisbrooke (1805 or 1806).[1] The scattered birthplace of their children show the vicissitudes of Army life. Their eld- est son, Francis James, was born in the Isle of Wight (about 1806), Henry in Sicily (1808), Eliza in Messina, Sicily, James in Palermo, Sicily, Maria at Malta, and Frederick Maitland in Edinburgh (1816). At one period of the Wars, Captain Francis Innes was sent to take possession of the Mediterranean Island of Lampedusa. After fighting in Spain, he was finally invalided home and arrived on the very day in 1815 that the people in England learned of the victory at Waterloo.

Settling in Scotland, the Captain's young family eventually lived at no. 3 Rankeillor Street, Edinburgh.

* Broken in health from his war service, Captain Francis did not live long after coming home and died in 1816, at the age of 40. Soon after his father's death Frederick Maitland Innes was born in Edinburgh, on 11th August 1816.

Written by Toney Innes

Prue sat by the fire all night. Mattie had brought a hot drink and food she could not touch and then had taken Baby Eliza, now fast asleep to her cot. It was no use begging Prue to go to her bed. She sat there seeing all the dreams that she and Francis had had for many years, dissolving one by one. He had promised to take her to his beloved Scotland and had pictured for her the shy deer roaming over the heather-clad purple hills, the beautiful little lochs and the castles and great abbeys and Edinburgh itself, loveliest of cities. He had spoken of the warm- hearted welcome his people, who had long ago forgiven the "unwise" marriage, would give them. But a few years earlier his parents had died. His elder brother, James, lived in the home, which Francis had described so well. Three storeys of substantial grey stone, the date 1700 cut into the outer walls. It was quite near the beautiful Tweed and the fine abbeys of the Border Country. On the wall of one of these were the names of his fore-fathers— still nearer was the Duke's magnificent castle, with its sixty two bedrooms.

On one of the castle archways was the coat of arms of the Innes family, with their Saxon motto, "Be traist" [true to God, King and Country] showing their Saxon ancestry. Near the river were the remains of Roxburgh Castle, where James II of Scotland was killed in August 1460. He had blown himself up experimenting with his first cannon.[iii] Yew trees there were seven hundred years old. He described the stables too—halfway up the drive, three sides of a square, with its yew hedge, a triumph of topiary art, cut into shapes of peacocks, balls, cups and a variety of animals. There would be ponies for Henry and Frank, just as there had been for Francis and his brothers. He had told Prue tales of the Borders and had promised to take her to see Flodden Field also to homes where the Bonnie Prince had stayed and to Holyrood where so much Scottish history was made. His eyes glowed and his face was full of pride as he spoke of his race and his home. Someday, he had promised, Prue and the children would know it all.

Now Prue sat still and frozen, unable to move. The fire was dying and poor Mattie, who did not know what to do, put her arm around her saying, "Dear Miss Prue, the children will want you so much tomorrow," and at last got her to bed where Prue lay, dazed, wide-eyed and sleepless till dawn.

Next day the regimental chaplain and two senior officers called to express their sympathy and regret. They mentioned that a boat would be leaving for Eng- land in a week's time and advised her to go, but would not hurry her and were very ready to help her in any way that she wished. Mrs. Maitland thought it wise to go too and take her girls to her son in Scotland. Mrs. de Lancey and Mrs. Rossi helped Mattie and Prudence acquiesced in everything. She was quite tearless and asked no questions but requested that she might take her husband's body to Scotland. But that could not then be done, the fighting was still going on and Francis and Colonel Maitland were buried where they fell under a cross bearing their names.

Mattie and Jim were to travel on the boat, too. No one told the children about their father. Mattie could not bring herself to do it. She adored the "Captain's" children and was very worried about Prue, who ate nothing and never spoke. At other times Mattie would have told the children not to bother their mother, but now she told them to run to her on all sorts of excuses. They were so young that they loved their mother without noticing anything, but Henry at eight, the image of his father, sensed something was wrong though he accepted Mattie's, "Your Mamma has a headache, Master Henry". He would bring a rose from his own garden to his mother. She would accept it but puzzled him by saying, "Thank you," without a smile. So unlike her.

One morning he and the other children were playing in the garden. Henry noticed a very lame soldier with a bandaged head going to the side door. This was not unusual. Francis and Prudence were always ready to help wounded men. But this man was carrying something. Henry went to the kitchen to Mattie. There was the man standing by the table on which he had placed his burden. He was not speaking, but opposite him Mattie stood, her apron up to her face, down which the tears were pouring. Henry watched for a moment. Then the man turned his head and Henry saw that he was MacWhirter, son of Francis' brother's gamekeeper and always his play fellow.

He had joined up when Francis went into the army and had never left him since. With the premonition of his Scottish blood, Henry knew that, fond as they all were of MacWhirter, it was not his wounds alone that caused Mattie's tears. So he looked quickly at the table and saw his father's sword, which he had often handled. He went to MacWhirter, saying, "Where is my father? Why is his sword here?" and was answered at once. "Master Henry, he sent it to you, you must take care of your mother now there is no one else. The Captain has given his life to keep you safe."The poor man was almost fainting, but he knew the courageous child to whom he spoke. Henry, his back and head very straight, was
so white that Mattie moved to him in alarm. But all he said was, "Mattie, must I tell her, or does my mother know?" and his lips quivered. She answered him, "Yes, she knows, Master Henry, but go to her and take his sword to her." Poor little eight-year-old. He was trying so hard to be like his brave father and MacWhirter, who

would willingly have given his life for Francis, handed him the sword and saluted. Carrying the heavy sword, Henry went straight to his mother and said, "Mamma, I know now, MacWhirter has just told me. He said to give this to you." Prue took it and put her arms around her brave little son who forgot to be a man and sobbed his heart out, at last breaking her calm, and as she wept with him, the poor things tried to comfort one another. MacWhirter and Mattie, who had lis- tened, were comforted too. Tears were so healing The other children were almost too young to realise their loss. Their father had been so often away, but Henry, a thoughtful boy, could remember many things of which they had talked and he knew that first of all, in his father's eyes, was his mother's happiness. So he did his best and kept the others amused when Prue's friends came to help her prepare for leaving.

Bloomlands

James Innes Senior, Frederick's uncle and guardian resided at *Broomlands*, Kelso from 1818 until his death in 1847. The house was part of the Roxburgh Estates and his residence while chamberlain to the Duke of Roxburgh.

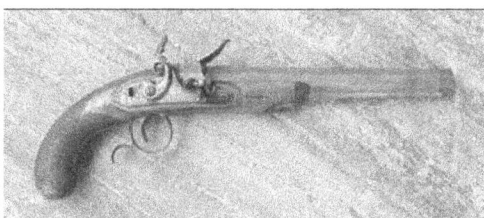

Innes Pistol

Captain Francis Innes' father Francis was from a long line of master Gun makers dating back
City of Edinburgh and lived at Leith Terrace. Frederick made
field

Frederick wrote,
'Of course, our natural pride inclines us to make the most of our ante-cedents, but candour does not prompt me to carry this feeling to any excess that would outrage veracity; my ancestors till a comparatively recent period belonged to the rank of master-tradesmen, burgesses of Edinburgh; my grandfather, and very likely great grandfather, followed
finally retired in the capacity
of Gunmaker to the King of Scotland, when he became Factor to the Duke of Roxburghe on the elevation of Sir James Innes

To Scotland

At last they were on board, Jim and Mattie too, and at the last moment, poor MacWhirter, who was too lame to be of any further use to the army and had been sent back to Scotland. So the children had plenty of nurses who loved them and Prudence could rest. She had written to her aunt in the Isle of Wight three days before and luckily had got the letter away. Then she wrote to James, Francis' brother. She told him she meant to take her children to her aunt so they might begin to know one another. She was sad that the Rector had lately died and she could not show them to him. After a month they would go to live in Edinburgh. Her aunt and little cousin, Felicity Jane, who had been only three at the time of the elopement, would be delighted to see them.

When they arrived, all the village came to welcome them. They were genuinely sorry to hear of Francis' death and they petted the children. Prue, Mattie and Jim felt they had come home. There were friendly faces everywhere when the children roamed about the pretty, pleasant village. But they had not been here long when Prudence realised she would soon have five, not four, children, to care for and she made up her mind that this one would be born on Scottish soil. She had written to her friend, Mrs. Maitland, asking her if she would look for a suitable home for herself and her children in Edinburgh.

Mrs. Maitland found a roomy, comfortable one, with quite a good garden, though not in the most fashionable quarter, but a little out of the city and healthy for the children. Accompanied by the faithful Mattie and Jim, who made a real sacrifice leaving their village, Prudence took her little brood off to their new home. Her Aunt and Felicity Jane promised to visit them there.

The twins, Charlie and Richard, now seventeen, had taken the first step in their career and were now midshipmen at Dartmouth, but wrote saying that on their first leave, they would come to see the children.

When the family had been almost three months in their new home, Henry looked out of the window and was surprised to see a shabby, thin man weeding their garden, although their mother had explained that she could not afford a gardener. So off he went to investigate and wasn't he delighted to find their old friend, MacWhirter, whom in great excitement he dragged into the warm kitchen. They all welcomed him with such joy that tears came into the poor fellow's eyes.

He was not really strong (weakened from wounds) and fifteen years in the army had put him out of touch with his boyhood friends. His parents were dead, he had no settled home nor near relations and 2/- a day pension and no uni- form did not go far towards providing a room and food. Now ,Mattie and the children were making him sit down in spite of his protests to the big- gest breakfast he had seen for months. Prudence came out and he had to confess that he had been unable to find either settled work or an abode. It was almost more than she could bear. She longed to offer him a job, but dared not. James Innes, Francis' brother, had been to see them and wealthy man as he was a widower with one son doing well at law,* he had somehow conveyed to her the fact that she must look twice at every penny she spent. Henry was looking at her imploringly so she said, "You must not go away now that you   have   found us,

MacWhirter. Henry needs help in the garden. Give us time to think," and went inside to rack their brains. James might help if appealed to. Mattie and Jim were thinking too. There was a good shed in the garden. She would scrub it and there was an iron bedstead that a former tenant had left. Some sacks could be filled with straw, as they had no spare mattresses. MacWhirter had his army blankets. They might find a few other things to help. Could he grow vegetables in the garden for the house and for sale? And come to them for his meals?

Jim gave him some of his precious tobacco which they smoked in the shed while they talked over army days. Jim had not yet got an artificial arm and was waiting patiently. He could not dig but there were other ways in which he could help MacWhirter. Prudence and the children were delighted. Of course MacWhirter must stay and he was only too happy.

Uncle James, of whom the children were in awe, came two or three days later and he objected at once. Did Prudence think her income could support old soldiers, because she had better think again! She said nothing and he went out and faced MacWhirter, found the garden much cleared and had a look at the shed, kept with an old soldier's neatness. Looked at the bed and was horrified. He said, "'Tut, tut, man, this won't do and you from a warm climate! What's your name? You're not old MacWhirter's boy? You are! Why, I remember. So you are!" and was off on a hundred reminiscences. "Of course you must stay here. I will order a decent mattress and good blankets at once." And was as good as his word. He shook hands with MacWhirter, leaving in his hand a banknote for Baccy, and saying, "Clothes will come soon. You should have come home."

Then he left, as happy as the children and Prue. He stirred up the shop he went to, to such purpose that in a short time a big hair mattress and two pairs of thick soft blankets arrived with feather pillows, Going straight home, he sent a box of his own half-worn tweeds and some warm shirts to share with Jim. From then on James took MacWhirter under his protection, never asking him to leave the Captain's children but making sure that he had plenty of suitable work and even keeping him from it by having long yams with him!

James was not mean, but he could be very trying! Perhaps he was lonely in his beautiful home but Prue was thankful he did not ask them to share it! He had a trying habit of always knowing best, but he was thankful that they had found a home without his help though inwardly he resented Mrs. Maitland choosing it. His

Jane Innes.
Broomlands. Ke[...]
Miniature on Ivo[...]

In 1816 James Innes Junior was only 13 years old and therefore not 'doing well at law' as stated here. His mother and spouse of James Senior was alive in 1816. She died in 1831. James Innes Senior's only daughter Jane, married in 1827, James Spittal Esq. a silk merchant in Edinburgh. His father later became Sir James Spittal, Lord Provost of Edinburgh. Jane died in childbirth in 1829.

At the time of Frederick Innes' birth the fifth Duke of Roxburgh was still alive. He died in 1823 at which time his young son became sixth Duke.

It is unlikely that the Duchess of Roxburgh ever met Captain Francis Innes. He left Edinburgh before 1804 and she married the Duke in 1807.

The text states indicates that in 1816 James Junior had already left the family home however. The census of 1841 shows him to reside at Broomlands with his father.

wife was dead and his only, very young daughter, married to Sir John R., had died with her baby at its birth. So now he centred all his attention on his very clever, only son and through his possessiveness, drove him away, after having his real love affair interfered with and spoilt, to leave home altogether and father and son seldom saw one another. The son was never to marry.

Perhaps all this had warped James' mind, but he was very clever and much respected. He was related to the very young fatherless Duke, for whom he was chamberlain, responsible for his estate, forests and all matters connected with them. Also, he had tactfully to restrain the Duchess, charming, but inclined to act beyond her powers and to forget that revenues from the estate were the property of her young son. She dearly loved to gamble and she did not like James suggesting economy at any time.

So he had a busy life, but his evenings in the quiet house were empty. His only pleasure there was his fine old library. Yet when he enjoyed a book, he wished his son were there to discuss it with him. Only his besetting sin, pride, prevented him from asking him to return. He would spend hours poring over the records of the Innes family, going back to Berowald, the Saxon to whom the name, Innes, had been granted.

The book which James loved was entitled, *The Historicall Account, Origine and Succession of the Family of Innes, collected from Authentick Writs in the Charter Chist of the Samen.* It was really a beautiful book, illuminated and showing the coat-of-arms of the various families with whom the Inneses had inter- married. It was written partly in Latin and partly in curiously spelt old English. It began with a beautifully illuminated letter S and this sentence, *"Since the Lord, among the greatest of his temporall blessings gives length of dayes to Man and a long standing to Families it may be holden as the part and gratitude due by Man to keep God's mercies in remembrance— it being a plain ingratitude to His memory to let His kindness in supporting a family for many ages in credit, drop into oblivion. This general consideration may be a good reason for families to give a clear account of themselves."*

There was one Innes, whose pride would not let him "give in" and for this man, James had a deep, secret sympathy. On page 36 the Innes Book described him.

"This man (tho' very gallant) had something of a particularity in his temper, was proud and positive in his deportment and had his law-sutes with several of his friends, one with Innes of Pethnok. This brought them both to Edinburgh in the year 1576, where the Laird, having met his kinsman at the Cross, fell in words with him for dareing to give him a citation and in choler, either stab'd the gentleman with a dagger or pistoll'd him. When he had done, his stomach would not let him fly but he walked up and down upon the spot, as if nothing could be quarrel'd, his friend's lyffe being but a thing he could dispose if, without count of it any other! However, this "intrepid deed" was described to the Earl of Morton, the Regent, who sent a guard who carried him away to the Castle. There he found his proud, rash action behooved to cost him his life. So he made a remission with the Regent, at the pryce of the Barony of Kilmallenock.

That evening he made merry with his friends at a collation and talking of the dearness of the Ransom the Regent made him pay, he vaunted that, had he his foot once loose, he would fain see what Earl of Morton durst come and possess his land. This was told the Regent and though it was spoken in drink, he put the sentence of death against him, causing his head to be cut off in the Castle, and then possest the estate."

James always felt this man was a kindred spirit; sometimes his loneliness made him so wretched he would have done anything to get his son back, but couldn't make himself take the first step. Now, tho' he pretended otherwise, he had been both pleased and excited that his youngest brother's widow had bought his children to Scotland. He thought of Francis with affection and had really felt his loss, but had often wondered what the widow of this "unwise marriage" would be like or the children, brought up in foreign lands. So when he first called on Prue in a critical frame of mind he had been pleasantly surprised to find, in a rather shabby sitting room a dignified, pretty and proud woman.

She had asked, "How are you, James? Would you like to sit near the fire?" and Henry, a good-looking boy, after shaking hands with him, moved forward the most comfortable, biggest chair. James sat down, feeling at once relaxed and at ease, and enquired about their journey over and if the house was comfortable, etc. Then Mattie, followed by the younger children, had brought in plum cake and wine and he had been favourably impressed by her pleasant face. The small girls had curt-syed and had held up their faces to be kissed by their uncle and Frank tho' shy had put out a hand to be shaken.

James had meant to give Prudence a hint that she must not rely on him too much, nor draw on him for unlimited funds, but how could he suggest this to this charming, dignified woman with her well-mannered children? There was no sign of extravagance in the house or its furnishings. He had been taken all over it on his second visit and noted the plainness, neatness and commonsense with which it was arranged and Prudence had refused help when he had asked was there anything he could do for her? "No," she'd said, "I think we have everything, thank you, James," and he'd recognised and respected a pride equal to his own. He had gone home to cudgel his brains. How could he help without hurting her? In the end he had done it through Mr. Darling, the family solicitor, who shortly wrote to Prudence, saying that Francis' father had placed in his hands a sum of money to be given to Francis, his wife and children, if they should come to live in Scotland.

Prudence never knew that Mr. Darling would have been more truthful if he had written "brother" instead of "father," but she was most grateful. She could buy the house and no longer have the nightmare of rent to face. There was even some over for Mr. Darling to invest and get enough interest to pay Mattie's wages. James had got into the habit of dropping in once a fortnight and was secretly so elated at being received affectionately by the children that he told the Duchess all about them. The Duchess remembered Francis, his happy manner and honest eyes, so though she was erratic, she was also kind-hearted and sent for her head gardener, telling him to send a basket of fruit and fresh vegetables for the children. "After all," she said, "they are my children's cousins and some day we must see them."

A Son Is Born

Prudence now felt more at home and was looking forward to the visit of her aunt and Felicity Jane, who were to come a fortnight before the new baby was due. James knew all about them and was on the verge of offering his carriage to meet them when the Duchess chose to play up. She was giving him a lot of trouble. She had decided she needed more money and without consulting him, had ordered the foresters to sell many of the finest trees in the young Duke's domain. James found out in time, but was obliged to get Mr. Darling to explain to her that she was acting against the law and had no

right to give orders about the estate! It was not pleasant for James to have to countermand her orders and he dared not leave unless everything was in order. He knew it was time and he felt anxious about Prudence. He could not concentrate on his books, went early to bed, but was unable to sleep, thinking of the young daughter he had lost. What would he do if the same thing happened to Prue? How could he care for her brood? So a very worried man rose early. There was no telephone to set his mind at rest. He ordered his horses and galloped all the way, arriving breathless and weary. Thank God, the blinds were up and Mattie opened the door smiling, as she said, "Yes, sir, the mistress is well", and ushered him into the parlour, where a bright faced woman, so like Prue, he knew it was her aunt, was talking to the doctor. He went straight up to her, with such agonised entreaty in his eyes, just saying, "Prudence?" that she guessed who he was and said gently, "Prudence has a little son". "But," he gasped, "but she, is she well?" and was told quickly, "She is very well, but only the doctor and I are allowed to see her for three days." He sat down, almost fainting and said, "I am so relieved. I am James Innes," and she made him drink coffee Mattie had just brought in. They had been up all night and needed it. She knew of James' losses and understood his anxiety and now she told him that Prue, considering all that she had been through in the last eight months, was wonderful, so happy that her little son, though small, was well. She was now asleep and a good nurse was with her. The aunt told James a pathetic thing. Prue had insisted that her husband's sword should be on her bed. Henry had told them that she always slept with it beside her and when the baby was coming she had fretted until they had brought it, whispering, "The baby must be brave, like his father."

James put his cup down. He said, "Is there anything she would like anything at all? Write them down, I will order them from Jenners' (the best draper)." The aunt was   a sensible woman.

She knew James to be a wealthy man and there were many needed things Prue was without, so she agreed at once. you have a rest here by the fire until break- fast is ready I will see what is needed and write a list," and went off to

The Baptismal Records of 1816 state that the child was baptised Frederick. Nowhere in the Scot- tish records. The name Maitland does not appear.

"If

discuss it with Mattie. James subsided into a comfortable old couch by the fire and had had quite a nap before being summoned to breakfast. He did not trouble to look at the list just tucked it into his vest pocket. The aunt and Mattie had enjoyed making the list. They had asked for a very complete layette and warm shawl for the baby, also for a soft, quilted dressing-gown and slippers and a pretty grey cashmere frock for Prue and give measurements. Mattie had dearly wanted to add a fur-lined cloak and a velvet bonnet, knowing how little that was fresh and pretty were in Prue's wardrobe, but the aunt said, "No, no. Mr. Innes is being very generous and my niece would not like us to be greedy." After breakfast, James had gone off to find MacWhirter, who was equally delighted and received an extra tip for tobacco, then he gave Mattie a sovereign, saying, "You three must all drink our little Scotsman's health" and was off, without waiting for thanks, but Mattie would not let him escape. She said quickly, "The mistress has no port. She will need something when she gets up, so I will get her some with this." "No, no," said James, who by this time was so excited, he felt he could go down town and get uproariously drunk. "An Innes, born not on foreign, but on Scottish soil! Of course, they must celebrate. No, no, woman. Put on the list a case of port and she shall have the best," which Mattie did, with great joy, showing the addition to the aunt, saying, "Mr. Innes comes quite often and the mistress always gives him a glass of wine, so it is time he gave her some." Mattie always looked after Prue's interest.

During the three days James had to wait, he told everyone his news, even the Duchess. He said, "A new clansman, your Grace," to which she had answered mischievously and colloquially, "But he has not put the noses of all the others out of joint, has he, James?" (Because of the relationship, he did not get the formal "Mr. Innes", though sometimes, he wished for it, when her friendliness made it difficult to refuse a not always reasonable request). So now he reddened, as he thought swiftly of Henry's smile and charm of manner and of young Frank, so serious and polite as he answered, "No, no, your Grace, but this boy was born in Scotland." She laughed, good naturedly when she said, "Well, James, this means I must call on his mother and welcome him. Let me know when she is well enough and tell Barton to send them fruit and vegetables every week." Thanking her, James went off to Edinburgh, very happy.

The children, whom kind friends had taken for a week, had returned and were thrilled to discover that they were now five, not four in number. They had such a lot to tell Uncle James.

The new brother was to be called Frederick Maitland after his father's C.O., Colonel Maitland, who had died with him.* The baby was small and red, but Mamma had said that he would grow. They had all been that size once! At any rate, he could make as much noise as any of them. They had heard him.

James went in on tip-toe to see Prue and when she smiled he was greatly relieved. Then he saw a little dark head resting on her shoulder and with his grey eyes, Frederick had black lashes and brows and a proper Innes nose, rather long and finely cut. He never had the good looks nor the fine physique of Henry, but he had his father's fine hands and as time went on, was meticulous in his dress, though his taste was too good to be foppish.

Not long after James' visit the Duchess proved as good as her word. In a few weeks, a handsome, crested carriage with beautiful matching bays and liveried men stopped at Prue's door. A footman came to enquire if Mrs. Innes were at home and able to receive the Duchess. Mattie, fresh and neat as usual, opened the door, and, too proud to let him guess that it was unusual for a Duchess to call, answered, "Yes, the ladies are at home". Then directly his back was turned she fled to the parlour where they were gasping out, "The Duchess". She was back at the door and then had time to straighten her cap before murmuring, "Yes, Your Grace. Please to come this way."

The "Ladies" rose quietly. Prudence advanced and all three curtsied as Prue said, "This is very kind. Your Grace," and then, with the little characteristic lift of her head, she introduced her aunt and asked would the Duchess care to sit near the fire? But, "No," the visitor said, "I want to meet our new clansman," and went to Frederick in his bassinet She studied him and added, "No wonder James is so pleased, he is like him," and then, laughing, to Prue. "A proper Innes, born in Scotland! But I must see the little foreigners, where are they?" Prue rang the bell, saying, "Mattie will get them. They are playing in our locked garden." This was a private square, owned conjointly by the houses around it. Henry and Felicity were quite sensible enough to be trusted with the care of the other children and MacWhirter took them back and forth over the road. Now, he went to get them.

Mattie told them nothing more than that a friend of Uncle James had come and wished to see them. So, while the Duchess sat and chatted, enjoying James' good port and plum cake (Mattie herself had made the latter), with towels and soap ready, she washed their hands and little rosy cheeks and combed their soft hair. Then telling the small girls not to forget to curtsy and the boys to bow, she took them to the parlour. Though their clothes were so plain and far from new, their manners were so charming and natural, their faces so smiling and fresh, that the Duchess was delighted.

Most certainly she was with Henry, he was so exactly like a portrait they had of his father, as a boy, with the same friendly honest eyes. She found herself unexpectedly shaken. She was glad she had sent the fruit and said she would continue to do so. Then she asked about the children's education and was told that Prudence had already arranged for Henry and Frank to attend school for the sons of fallen officers. It was well known and already a very clever young cousin, Henry Mortimer Innes, who was there had written and recited in Latin a welcoming speech to the Royalty who had visited Edinburgh.

At twelve, Henry was to go to Dartmouth College to join the R.N., but Prue thought Frank would be likely to take law. The two little girls, Eliza and Maria, would be chiefly educated at home by their mother or a governess while Freder- ick's future was still to be considered. James had great plans for Frederick which he had not yet confided to anyone, of sending him to school at Kelso so that he could often see and keep an eye on him. The Duchess parted from them in the most friendly manner, saying, "You must all come and spend a day with us," and they did.

A few years later Prue decided to leave Frank and Frederick in Mattie's care and take the two small girls to London. Felicity Jane, now grown up, was to be married and wanted Eliza and Maria as bridesmaids at the wedding. They were dressed in the latest, most picturesque fashion in wide, rather short pink organdie frocks with off-the-shoulder sleeves, three or four frilly white petticoats and long, starched, white pantalettes ending in lace frills, tied with narrow black ribbon at the ankles; their sandals, mittens and the hanging bow on the Leghorn hats were blue. Prue touched their soft ringlets and could not help looking at them with motherly pride. The style had already been taken up in London and they saw a number of other small girls like themselves, although when they returned the fashion had not yet reached Edinburgh.

One day Prue decided to take them in all their glory, to see a friend who would be very interested. On the way they stopped at a draper's where Prue wanted to see some tweeds. The shop assistant was busy showing them to her. It was rather early for the usual customers so the shop was very quiet. Maria and Eliza were roaming about looking at things and their mother too absorbed to notice, when suddenly there was a commotion and shouting just outside the shop door. Prue and the assistant looked round anxiously, Prue saw that little Eliza, who was timid, was hiding behind a bale of silk, but at the door, gazing at the sky and apparently oblivious of all confusion was Miss Maria. She was taking no notice whatever of about twenty street Arabs who were pointing at her shouting, "Lassies, lassies, i breeks" (girls with trousers—shorts and slacks had not been thought of then). Horrified Prue took the little girls to the back of the counter, while the shop assistant hurriedly locked the door and let them out the back. [iv]

This little incident showed the girls' characteristics Eliza was always shy, while Maria, who became a beauty, ruled everyone around her, in such a way that none resented her. But she was fortunate in marrying a man with a sense of humour. She had a daughter Jane, very like her mother in every way. Jane married the scholarly chaplain of an Oxford College and "for their own good," never allowed a child of hers to dream through life. Her daughters were happily and well married and her three sons successful. The first, a Canon of Salisbury Cathedral, the sec-ond in the Marines, was in 1918 in command at Deal and the third, remarkably clever, gained honours and distinctions for his work in In-dia.

The Census of 1861 and 1871 show Frank to be a retired clerk in the Inland Revenue. The text also states that his wife was several years older than him but in the 1871 Cen- sus shows Frank was 65 years and his wife Ann

As Prudence had thought, her son Frank was very clever and studious and though shy, became one of the most prom-ising young barristers in Edinburgh, but he was also absent-minded. He did not marry early and did not realise that time was passing, until Henry, on leave, brought his charming wife and three sons, James, Edward Selby and Ashley to see Edinburgh. They lived in England. Frank enjoyed their society immensely and felt so lonely when they left that he gave se- rious thought to matrimony. He was always more serious than the others and now he decided to act at once. He was thinking of a young sister of a widow, a clever, wordly-wise woman, whom he had often met in society.

Nothing he did was spontaneous—the polished speeches, which he made for law-suits, were most carefully prepared, and now, he thought, "I must put into words all that I feel, I hope that she will be interested." So one day, looking his smartest and conning over the words in which he meant to propose, he went to her home and enquired of the maid. "Is Miss S. at home?" and was shown into the drawing-room to find the widow alone. Nervous at the thought of proposing and also because the sister delayed coming in (she was out in the garden), Frank be-came almost speechless.

The widow made several attempts to begin and continue a conversationbut it was no use so, at last, she said, "Is some- thing the matter, Mr. Innes?" and hardly knowing what he was doing, the polished, well-prepared words of his proposal rolled off his tongue and he was adding, "The lady I have in mind, is your sister," when the as- tute widow burst out, "Oh, Mr. Innes, how wonderful of you! I really had no idea that you entertained such thoughts of me! I have felt so lonely since my poor Edmund departed, that I can only accept your beautiful proposal with a grateful heart. "Poor Frank! His utter shyness and the fact that his breath was taken away prevented speech. He was caught. Just then the sister came into the room and the news was immediately given to her by the widow, who said, "We are two lonely people, Frank and I, Isobel, so we will not have a long engagement. He has made me so happy." Next day, Frank found everyone in Edinburgh had been told and feeling bewildered, he resigned himself. The young sister expressed no opinion. Perhaps, after all, a carefully- prepared speech might not have appealed to her! If Frank had had dreams he had to forget them. He had provided himself with a good housekeeper and dinner- party hostess but she was several years older than he, very possessive and rather jealous of his relations and he could not provide Henry's children with cousins.

When his brothers on leave suggested coming to spend a night with him he found himself having to make excuses. His wife would invariably become ill and in spite of a good staff (cook, etc.), would say, "No, Frank, it is too much to ask. I should love to have your brothers, but they should not worry you, and I, myself, do not feel equal to visitors, they tire me so". When he protested, "It is for a very short visit, my love, and sailors make no trouble," she would shake her head in a most determined manner. "No, Frank, they must make some other arrangements. We have quite a number of engagements ahead and cannot alter them. Really, your family seem most thoughtless and inconsiderate. They should not disturb you. Don't they realise what important work you do?"

So, having been weak to begin with, he would give in for the sake of peace and write sorrowfully to his brothers asking them to stay at a nearby hotel, at his expense and when he could, he would plead extra work at the office or slip off to spend a happy evening with them. But they did not like it, even though he spoke of his wife's "delicate health," and after a couple of years, made excuses for not coming, so their intercourse was entirely through letters. In the family, they always spoke of "Poor Frank and his precious wife". be more lively, Frank. You are getting as dry as your law books!" and never seemed to realise it was the result of her own work, separating him from those he loved

Frank became more absorbed in his profession, as the years passed and though that brought success, his wife was not satisfied. She would say, "You might

16 Heriot's School

Frederick Maitland Innes spent his early childhood in Edinburgh following the footsteps of his father, older brother Henry and other members of the family by attending Heriot's school. His uncle, James Innes, became his legal guardian early in Frederick's childhood. James was a Writer to the Signet and Factor to his relative the Duke of Roxburghe. He also managed the Duke's estates at Kelso on the River Tweed near the English border once described by Sir Walter Scott as "the most beautiful, if not the most romantic village in Scot- land". Most of Fredericks' boyhood was spent at Kelso, with his Uncle James. From "Broomlands" he walked daily through the groundsof *Floors Castle* to the Kelso Grammar School. *Floors Castle* was built in 1718 for the 5th Earl of Roxburghe with both families' Arms on the pillars of the castle gates.

Uncle James had a fine library at "Broomlands", and there young Frederick read and studied, supplementing his school studies and acquiring the knowledge and love of good literature which he retained throughout his later years. As he grew into adulthood life at Kelso must have seemed monotonously dull and the impetuous Frederick longed for the adventures of youth. At 18 he ran away to join the Eng- lish forces then in action in Spain only to be promptly discharged and returned home through his Uncle's intervention.

Down but not out Frederick resumed his studies in Law until two years later his travel itch resurfaced, leaving his Uncle again, went to London and booked his passage to Van Diemen's Land. He sailed on the 362 ton "bark" *Derwent* (A. Riddle, Master), bound for Hobart Town with general cargo and passengers, the latter including his Scottish friends "Captain Scott, 2 sons and 1 daughter". The little ship left London on 18th October 1836 and, after just under four months at sea, reached Hobart Town on 4th February 1837.

Researched and written by Toney Innes

Footnote: *James Scott, originally from Scotland, was a well-respected surveyor, explorer and politician a prominent member of the Tasmanian community. More information about the life of J R Scott available from Neil Smith Australian Dictionary of Biography, Volume 6,(MUP), 197

When Lysbeth and Fredrick settled back in V.D.L. in the 1840s they lived for a time at "Verulam" near St. Leonards but later they went to "Woodmount" for- merly called Mona Vale, which belonged to Lysbeth. Frederick chiefly occupied himself in journalism. Then in 1856 the first Parliamentary Assembly was held in Hobart. Frederick had always been intensely interested in politics and the govern- ment of the country and often wrote articles on these subjects. Everyone knew of his interest and a number of settlers surrounding them drew up and signed a petition asking him to act as their representative and when a poll was held, he easily topped it.

The whole family moved to "Cottage Green" in Hobart, stayed there for a short time and then went to "Newlands," a lovely stone house, surrounded by 32 acres of gar- den, lawn, shrubbery and orchard in Newtown. It was delightful for a large family with room for archery, croquet and other amusements. There were good stables too, a great consid- eration as they all loved to ride. The house walls were very thick and solid and the win- dows had shutters inside, as well as out, in case bush-rangers appeared, although they never did. Tho' Lysbeth loved the country she had suffered much from want of water and pipes to lay it to her house so it was a great

Figure 25 Sarah Elizabeth

relief to be where she had all she wanted. The children too loved New- lands, but as soon as they were old enough each one went to boarding school. There was always the garden to come back to and Hanks gardener an ex-Tommy and who lived in their cottage with his family, was a great character and amusement to them. One day the boys saw him labelling cases of their apples "H.R.H." and pro- tested. A Royal Duke was visiting Hobart at the time so they said, "You are not giving him all our apples, are you Hanks?" He was most indignant "Surely," he said to them, "you must know it stands for "Horchard Red H-apples."

The two elder girls, Catherine and Elizabeth, were often sent to see their Aunt Kate and grandfather at Eastbourne which gave all concerned great pleasure. Small Catherine was musical but when they lived at Woodmount, having no piano, Lysbeth had taught her to read her notes and exercise her fingers by practising on a table. At Eastbourne she could use Kate's piano and a blind tutor from Avoca was engaged to give her lessons. She learned surprisingly well and all her life she played delightfully. On the other hand Elizabeth could not learn. She was her grandfather's companion, they would set off in a buggy with the inevitable plum cake and bottle of wine in case they lost their way, and go off for the day visiting a neighbour or having a look at the fences. She was very quick and like her mother had learned to read well at four years old.

Her grandfather instilled into them his ideas of a "lady's education". She must learn to speak and understand French; study music to give pleasure, not only to herself, but to others; always step lightly; and most important never break a promise. These simple rules were always drilled into the girls andoccasionally were applied in an amusing way as when Catherine put a perfectly new pair of shoes into the fire. Her careful mother had sent her a heavier than usual pair for wet weather but as Catherine said, "They would never step lightly." As well as everything else there were always ponies for the children at Eastbourne so they rode regularly and were at home with horses.

When the two little girls were considered old enough they were sent to a small Launceston Boarding School kept by a dear old French woman. Her husband had dinner with her and the girls, every day asking her the same question, "Is this Carolina or Patna rice my love?" The girls learnt to speak French with ease and met and made some very nice friends, country girls like themselves.

Lysbeth enjoyed the social life of Hobart. Frederick was very much occupied with his parliamentary work and not so fond as she was of parties but he would reluctantly accompany her. His love of literature and the fine library that grew on the walls of Newlands drew many kindred spirits especially among the Governors and their wives. Lysbeth said once "If it were the choice of doing without a new or rare book or his dinner, I am sure he would do the last."

He had all the best of the contemporary writers, as well as English, French and Latin classics, studied them well and the eloquent speeches he made on occasions were made more interesting by the appropriate quotations he used. As a member of Parliament he received no salary and compared with latter day Ministers very little when he held office,

but his search for pleasure in a good book was that of a keen terrier after a

*The real and confronting story of Jane Franklin's involvement with aboriginal children is now well documented.

bone! It was well that Lysbeth could share in his pleasure, tho' she would sigh sometimes when the growing expenses of her family were not easy to meet.

Newlands

Lysbeth once told an amusing incident in her early married life when Sir John (Franklin) was Governor and Lady Franklin cherished the belief that, if trained early enough, young aboriginal girls would behave exactly as their white contemporaries, so she kept a few with her for some months then decided to give a dinner-party and launch them in society. The dinner itself went off well. They spoke very little and evidently remembered all they had been told, their bright eyes, snow white teeth and happy smiles made them attractive. Their dress had, in the prevailing fashion, high waist, short sleeves and very full skirts. When Lady Franklin and the other ladies present went to the drawing room, the girls followed and were sitting down, as requested, when they upset everyone's gravity completely.

With extended hands, each carefully took the hem of her skirt and raised it to her ears but instead of the four frilly petticoats underneath with which each had been provided, there was nothing at all. Nothing but brown skin! Much to their surprise they were hustled out of the room before the gentlemen could join them! Civilization was very puzzling. They had understood that crumpled dresses looked shabby and they had been careful with these best frocks and had not sat on them!

Yet no one seemed pleased!*

TRANSPORTATION OVER

When the agitation over anti- transportation first began in the country, Fredrick had supported Governor Denison in deciding that cheap, convict labour was necessary for finishing public roads and buildings but on Earl Grey's sending out more and more convicts, against the expressed wishes of free settlers, he changed his views and added his signature to the petition sent to the Home Government by those who objected to their children growing up amongst such sights. In 1853 the settlers got their wishes. Transportation ceased. Church bells rang out throughout the land and thanksgiving services were held. The children were feasted and a fireworks display was held.

In 1866, Federick Maitland Innes was the member for Morven later called Evandale, and William Thomas Napier Champ was the first Premier. In 1857, F. M. Innes was the Colonial Treasurer. His uncle James, died in Scotland so he had been sent the "Innes Book" (already in several wills) also a beautiful silver loving cup given to his uncle by the Hammermen of Edinburgh.* Like his uncle he was often amused and interested when he read the stories of his ancestors. Many of them had several daughters for whom marriages had been arranged from their birth. But at one time the Laird's sixth daughter evidently had a mind of her own and so the book recorded "She married herself, without her parents consent, to a gentleman of the name of Sutherland."

Lysbeth retained her childhood characteristics, loving, impetuous and warm-hearted and she could not suffer snobs gladly. One fine day she was walking into town when she was joined by an acquaintance, for whom she had little liking, knowing her to be a social climber and not a nice one.

The families' fortunes and material serenity was greatly disturbed by the economic depression of the period. The whole of VDL was affected by the late 1830's recession in England See more in Volume Two.

She was very flattering to Lysbeth, who did not appreciate it and found it difficult not to be curt in response. On the way they met a shabby, tired-looking woman. Lysbeth stopped to speak to her enquiring for her child whom she had heard was ill. Then she promised to send him some fruit and a delicacy. As they parted and almost before the mother was out of hearing Mrs. S.C. said "Oh my dear Mrs. Innes, do you think you should waste time talking to those people? Isn't it rather beneath your dignity to talk to people like that? Shouldn't you consider your position?" Lysbeth did not answer for a moment, then she looked at her with such contemptuous eyes as she answered. "My position? I have none, if I am always thinking of it. Her child is ill and was silent. Mrs.S.C. found it convenient to leave at the first turn off.

On another occasion Lysbeth had a funny little experience. She was out in her front garden when she heard a shout and saw some stones thrown. The big iron gates were pushed open and a ragged-looking thin youth rushed in. She recognised him as "Daft Jimmie", a poor simple boy. She said "What is the matter Jimmie?" but he was too frightened to answer. There was blood on the thin hand shading his face and he fled to the dividing orchard wall, leaning against it. Then outside she saw two or three larrikins laughing as if it were a great joke so she said "What are you doing? You big bullies, you should be ashamed of yourselves." But they said "Well, missus, 'e was stealing your apples and we caught 'im at it." She looked at the poor thing still shaking and trying to hide his face and at the larrikins and thought shrewdly, "You mean he got in just before you," but she said, "Of course Jimmie can have one and what is more, he can get one for each of you, but you must be friendly to him." They were quite pleased now and promised not to tease him again as he brought the apples to them.

But Lysbeth had a devoted slave for life, so anxious to do little things for her it was almost trying. One of his ways was to go to the front door and ask for "the great, the Honourable Mrs. Innes" and ask would she buy his (invisible) chips. On being told "Yes" and if he took them to the kitchen he would be given a shilling he immediately went to the back and without a "by your leave" helped himself to their wheelbarrow, went to their orchard, filled it with bits of wood and called at the kitchen grinning with joy and asking for his shilling! The whole thing amused them so, that he was never disappointed, but he, was harmless and honest as far as he understood and often helped Hanks in the garden.

On one occasion he really did cause Lysbeth some embarrassment. She and Frederick had driven to the Cathedral for the wedding of a well-known girl. The usual interested or curious crowd waited in the street to see the bride arrive. Suddenly there was a little commotion. There was Daft Jimmy, mowing right and left waving his arms, shouting, "Make way, make way for the great, the Honourable Mrs. Innes". Poor Lysbeth! The crowd laughed as she got out hastily and fled, scarlet-cheeked, into the Cathedral, Jimmy bowing before her.

In 1857 F. M. Innes was Colonial Treasurer. The historian, Major Fenton, recorded, the "Treasurer Mr. Innes, made a masterly financial statement", and in 1863 Mr. Henty retired and Mr. Innes became Colonial Secretary. In 1865, three Commissioners were appointed to form a Railway Co. and Frederick Maitland Innes was one of them. In 1869, on the death of his neighbour, W. E. Nairn,[xvi] F. M. Innes was elected President of the Legislative Council.

*Frederick's Uncle James Senior died at *Broomlands* in 1847. His Testament makes no mention of the Innes Book or the Silver Loving Cup. The book was gifted to Frederick by his elder brother Francis James Innes in April 1854 and he was left the latter by his cousin James Innes Junior who died in 1876. His uncle left him with naught. (Toney Innes – unpublished)

From Her Grace the Duchess of Roxburghe To Mrs Francis Innes, Holywood-house, And from her, to her Grandsons, Fran- cis and [?] Innes.

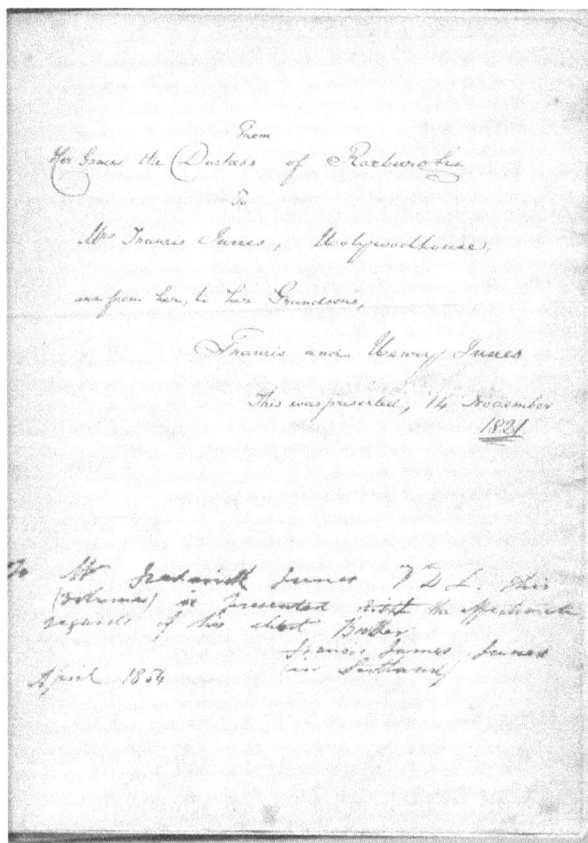

This was presented, 14th November 1821 To Mr Frederick Innes VDL. This [?] is presented with the affectionate regard of his [?] Brother April 1854 Francis James Innes

F.M. Innes circa 1840

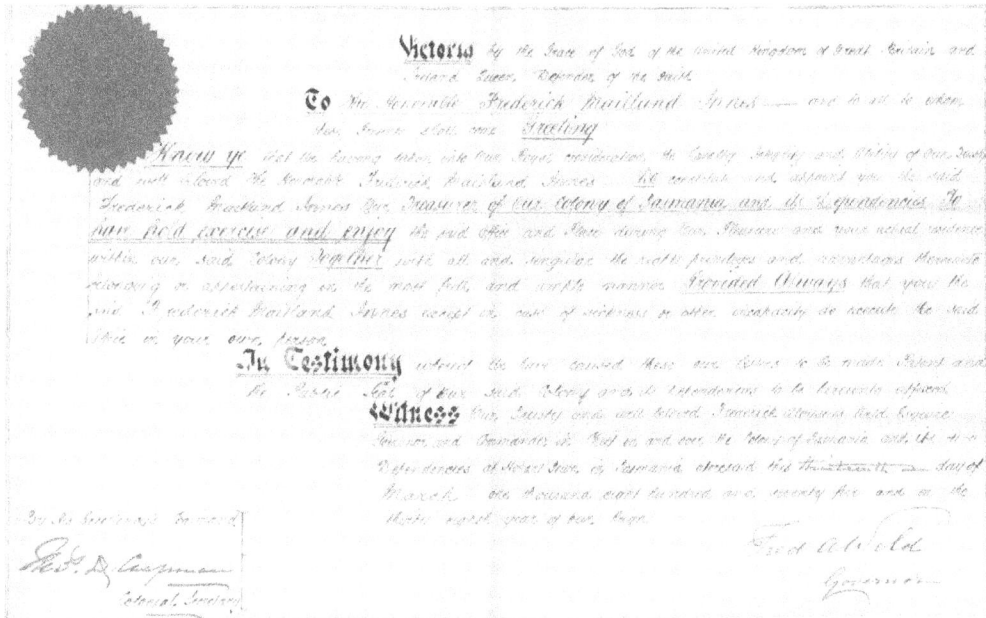

Figure 43 Proclamation of F M Innes as Treasurer

DEATH OF HUMPHREY GREY

17 Grey Family Vault at Avoca By Richard
Chuck

GREY.—On 4th May, at his residence, Eastbourne,
Avoca, Humphrey Grey, Esq., aged 88 years.

In 1868, much to everyone's regret, Lysbeth's father, Humphrey Grey, had
died.[xvii] The Tasmanian papers said of him:—
*"He was engaged on the side of loyalty in the Irish Rebellion of 1798. He how-
ever, retired early and with his family immigrated to this Island and on the ship was*

the no less respected colonist, Aleander Clerke, Esq., of Mountford. Mr. Grey selected land in the Avoca district, where he was early distinguished for his industry and probity. Of great intelligence and warm hospitality, he brought his career to a close with unimpaired mental faculties, at an age seldom attained by humanity, being over 88 years."

The Governor at that time was Colonel Gore-Browne. He and his wife shared Frederick's love of literature and often came to Newlands to discuss books and poems. As Jane Austen put it, "Abundance of civilities passed on all sides."

When Mrs. Gore- Browne returned to England, she wrote;

How graphically you and Newlands came to our minds last Sunday when my husband and I spent a day with the Martineaus at their lovely home near Windsor. It was very pleasant among the old oaks of the park to recall the view from your verandah and to repeat passages from your books, but it was very sad that for the future, these things can live only in memory. I want you to know that the never ending bustle and glitter of this busy world of London seems to make the memory of valued friends stand out in bold relief.

Colonel Gore-Browne wrote soon after;

Lord Clarendon's death has made a great sensation for he was very much be- loved, and I presume that the Colonies will not regret the departure of Lord Granville, who, (though he is the blandest man in conversation) writes somewhat drily.

I have accepted the Governor- ship of Bermuda for six months only. I had hoped not to go abroad again, but the act of Parliament is positive that a Governor must serve eighteen years before he can get a full pension. I have served 17 years, 6 months and 11 days, so I am going to Bermuda to complete the 18 years. My wife and Steward go with me, but we leave the children at home, and I hope to be back again before April 1871. Lord Granville has been very civil in doing this for me, so I must not complain of the trouble of another voyage out. I trust it will be my last. We are, as you suppose, in a bustle, so will conclude with kindest remembrances.

P. Gore-Browne.

Elizabeth still kept up correspondence with relations in England, and she was very pleased in 1872 to get a letter from Sir John Quain, Cavendish Square, Lon- don.

18 Image of original letter

My dear Elizabeth,
I do not wish that you should learn exclusively from the newspapers the change that has taken place in my fate and fortunes, I have been appointed Judge of the Court, of the Queen's Bench. It is one of the peculiarities of my profession that one has to wait a long time before promotion to the highest places can be hoped for, and many, many, hope to the end in vain. I

have been more fortunate and have brought my career at the Bar to an end in a most happy manner. The only regret that attends it, is that my dear mother did not live to see it. I shall be glad to learn that Innes, yourself and all your family are well. Pray remember me to them and to all my Tasmanian relations. I only hope that Innes continues to hold the important post of President of the Legislative Council. Don't forget your relations in the Old Country.

> Humphrey's wife Catherine Grey (nee Mahony) died many years before him in 1847. Courier (Hobart, Tas. : 1840 - 1859), Wednesday 10 November 1847, page 2
>
>
>
> At Eastbourne on the 5th instant, CATHERINE, the wife of Humphrey Grey, Esq. th year of her age. She departed this life with a good hope of a joyful resurrection through the merits of her Redeemer

Holidays[xviii]

> On a lighter note Humphrey also managed to go on a holiday some years earlier in **1856** to Falmouth Hotel and clearly enjoyed the **experience** to such an **extent** that he and his fellow guests provided Mr. **Pineo** with some public praise, probably the **equivalent** to modern day web reviews.

TO MR. G. PINEO.

SIR,—We, the undersigned visitors at the Falmouth Hotel, are much gratified to testify our high appreciation of the exertions you have made to promote our amusement during our stay at Falmouth, and also to give our testimony to the excellent arrangements to secure us every possible comfort.

Having thus experienced your assiduous attentions, we cannot but commend your establishment to the patronage of the public, and trust that yourself and Mrs. Pineo will long continue in your present position to the advantage of yourselves and those who may your future guests.

We beg to remain, sir,
Your obedient servants,
Adam Jackson, Williamswood.
Joseph Brown, Fingal.
Charles Hill Harrison, Campbell Town.
Frazer S. Crawford.
Arthur John Harrison.
Humphrey A. Gray.
William Jackson, Ross.
George, J. C. Amos.
Johana Jackson.
Selina E. Ward.
Henry G. Archiball, Rose Garland.
Robert Cameron, Lundava.
Robert M. Cox
Falmouth, July 18.   232

> William and James died many years earlier in 1848 and 49 respectively perhaps as a result of broken hearts and failed ambition.
> See volume two box eighteen: death of William and James gray

19 H.E. Charles Ducane, Esqre visiting the squadron, River Derwent, Tasmania 1871 unknown artist Allport Library and Museum of Fine Arts

THE FLYING SQUADRON

In 1870 Frederick had received a letter from his brother Henry saying that his second son, Edward Selby Innes, a lieutenant of Marines, on board H.M.S. Scylla, one of the ships of the Flying Squadron, now on a five-year cruise of the British Dominions, would soon arrive in Tasmania.

All Hobart became highly excited. Twelve ships of the line, fully rigged, all sails and flags flying, came floating up the beautiful Derwent. At once the gayest season was in full swing. Government House and all society leaders issued invitations to balls and dinner parties but even more than these pleasures, Edward Selby and his friends loved to spend a day or more at Newlands, and other kindred homes. The girls and boys loved their coming. The sailors enjoyed the taste of home life which they missed so much at sea. They loved the garden and orchard, "Aunt Elizabeth's" motherliness and the chance to ride on the cousin's horses. Governor Du Cane had succeeded Colonel Gore- Browne. He liked to keep up almost regal state. It was quite a thrill to go to Government House and to be waited on by scarlet-liveried, powdered- haired footmen. St. James did not seem far away! Margaret, Edward's tiny charming cousin, clad in much-flounced tarlatan, worn over five petticoats, made her debut at Government House, entering the ballroom on the red-coated arm of the six foot Edward. With the navy ashore, Hobart was a happy, light- hearted,

> *Tarlatan is a kind of thin, transparent muslin often used for dresses
> The poem mentioned is from Thomas Moore 1779 – 1852 'The Fire- worship- pers';
> I never nurs'd a dear gazelle, To glad me with its soft black eye, But when it came to know me well And love me, it was sure to die.

community, yet the girls were not extravagant. For balls, their frocks, of yards and yards of tarlatan were hand- sewn by themselves at home but their fresh complexions and happiness made them charming, so it was not surprising that several young sprigs of visiting English nobility lost their hearts entirely.

Engagements and even marriages, after the fleet's six weeks stay, followed. They were all very quick, quoting appropriately from the poets. For instance if a love affair went awry a girl would philosophically remark to her friend, "Well didn't Pope say, 'I never loved a dear gazelle but it was sure to die?'" and they would laugh.* No one ever made a "tactless" remark. That would constitute was a *faux pas*. It was a fashion at Government House to mingle French phrases in ordinary conversation.

The Flying Squadron
This was a time of extraordinary change for the Royal Navy. The future was now clear, sail would soon be a relic of history as steam power and metal took pride of place in the design of British warships. Even with the disastrous sinking of the Captain there would be no turning back and in 1873 the HMS Devastation was launched, the first ever steam only bat- tleship and proved to be a powerful weapon in the British Fleet. Added to this Gladstone, the Prime Minister, had embarked on a program of social reform which required funds resulting in the reduction of the Navy from 17000 down to 10000 men. Perhaps by way of consolation the Lords of the Admiralty organised an around the World tour of the Colonies and other nations in 1869.
Read more in volume two box nineteen: ships and social life

Flying Squadron in the River Derwent[xix]

Flying Squadron in the Derwent River, Hobart Town, Jan- uary 7th, 1870

Apart from dancing and music their chief pleasures were archery and riding and the girls were generous to one another, the one riding habit would not alone be shared by a sister, but on occasions by a friend. For riding-parties were very popular. But though the sailors could walk with dignity on rolling decks, they did not seem to feel at home on trotting horses! A smart young officer might call on a fair damsel and make, humbly, a request that she would accompany him on a ride. If she agreed, she would mount her horse, side- saddle, in her flowing habit, and holding the reins firmly in a tiny gauntleted hand, would sit up as if she were born in the saddle. She was charmingly ready for a canter or race but what could she do when her escort in a very short time unwillingly lost his cap trying to gasp out compliments on her prowess, while he bounced up and down like a sack of potatoes (tho' given the quietest steed) and often finished by sliding into space? However, there were no serious accidents and perhaps the horsemen enjoyed the sympathy they got, for their "heroic efforts."

The girls had many a laugh amongst themselves over these excursions. Lieutenant Carr of H.M.S. Clio wrote, "I was fortunate enough to get leave and spent most of it riding and driving, first-rate fun! We had some falls but not serious accidents. The Clio gener-ally comes out well. It is a regular 'horseman ship' (N.B. joke)." He was evidently much affected by

HMS Clio in Hobart public domain

the beauty of Tasmanian girls, for he also said, "I intend to give up comic songs and devote myself to sentiment!" There was a constant exchange of likenesses as the neat little photographs of the day were known. Every persuasion would be brought to bear on a young lady, to get her to part with hers, and her album, in turn, would be filled with those of "beggars" in uniform.

Elizabeth took her two young daughters to a dance on the Scylla, but was implored by twelve other young things (and their Mammas) to chaperone them too, and with Lysbeth's usual generosity agreed. So she arrived on board with fourteen beauteous maidens, so overwhelming Edward, who had expected his cousins that he could not remember their names and introduced them enmasse to his ship-mates, as my cousins.

Each young lady would be the owner of an autograph book, usually clad in beautiful, rose coloured morocco. In it, very finely drawn, would be a card with the name of one of the ships and surrounding it, at all angles, were others, on which each of the personnel of that particular ship, would write his name. Or, there might be an acrostic, beautifully illuminated, printed in Old English, by the artistic member of the mess, often original, with the first letters of the first word in each line helping to form the name of the fair one! There would be the usual delicate little drawings and water colours.

In one book was a delightful picture of a young lady, clad in the pink crinoline of the period, with lace-frilled pantalettes showing below. She had the usual blue rib boned Leghorn hat and golden ring-lets, but she was evidently petrified with horror. Her enormous blue eyes were open to their widest and her rosebud mouth set in a tiny 'O'! She stood on the borders of a lake which was almost

Edward Selby INNES September 1844 and the son of Barbara and Henry Innes (Malta Family History). He had a long and distinguished career covered with water lilies, but, most conspicuous amongst them was a pair of smart stripe-trousered legs sticking straight up into the air! No sign of the remainder of the owner. This touching effusion was captioned, "Oh! those darling water lilies!"

The Flying Squadron's visit to Hobart was made notable by their eventful return home journey. The British Government for some time had been discussing mutual trade exchanges with Japan but the Japanese distrusted the entrance of any foreigners, for any reason, into their country. By way of beginning, the Emperor of Japan had been asked might a British fleet make a friendly visit and call upon him? He agreed and the Flying Squadron, again all sails and flags flying, reached port! They were received by a party of politicians and Japanese officers, who were armed to the teeth. These men looked for all the world like hedgehogs walking upright because they bristled with swords and guns of all types, which clanked and bumped like saucepan lids. The weight must have been considerable. Evidently, they intended to strike awe into the visitors hearts. So the chosen British officers, headed by their Admiral, went ashore, completely unarmed leaving all dirks, pistols, swords etc., on board, in the hope of inspiring trust.

Then, surrounded by much clanking and noise they were escorted to the Emperor's Palace. Here they were received with low bows, many smiles and polite speeches and were treated to, and expected to enjoy, such an enormous banquet that they wondered if they would survive it and had some difficulty in disguising from their hosts, who accompanied them back to the ships, their intense relief in reaching their cabins with some dignity!

There was great sorrow when the ships left Hobart, both on the part of the hosts and visitors. It had been such a happy, successful tour, never forgotten by either.

Letters from Edward Innes

Edward wrote from almost each port they reached, easily and well, his letters were most interesting. The first was from Columbia:

"Your letter only reached me this week. Took four solid months on the road! I hope mine was not so long, if so, the long sea voyage of the Flying Squadron must bear the blame. We have been stationed at Esquimalt [the harbour of Victoria]. The Colony is about to enter the

Canadian Confederation, it being still at the time a Crown Colony and one of the intended improvements when they join it is to be a railway right across from Canada to the Pacific, so that England can be quite independent of the American Pacific Railway.

We shall have a short road of our own from England to Japan and China. Esquimalt is about four miles from Victoria, and as the shooting and fishing is good, the amusement during the summer months consists of picnics, taken on the "arm," as it is called, an inlet of the sea, about 3 miles long, and in some parts very narrow, about 330 yards. In fact, it is in a very pretty part, thickly wooded on each side. At one spot near the end, a speculative genius built a shack and many of the picnic parties adjourn there, towards evening and wind up with a dance. The picnics sensibly never start until towards the cool of the evening. I do not know what I would have done, if I had not had my little skiff. It is wonderful and makes me independent and salmon fishing is a great amusement.

We use an affair called a 'spoon-bait,' a thing like the cup part of a spoon below, and above which are fixed four large hooks. It is silvered on one side and coppered on the other, and when fixed to a line with a swivel, revolves when drawn through the water. The foolish fish, seeing something bright darting through the water, makes a dash for it, and is caught. The Indians, who always live entirely on fishing, are- very clever at spearing them and for I/- one gets a 15 or 20 lb. fish. In a net, when we are at a particular spot, we have caught over 400 lb. weight at a haul. I am having a delightful change, living on shore and only go on board from 9 to 11.30 a.m. The wardroom is being painted, white with gold molding. On the panels are pasted coloured pictures from the 'Illustrated London News,' crystal varnished so that the colours do not run. My cabin is French grey with a vermillion stripe.

"Do not be surprised to hear that we have left the Pacific. If nothing turns up to alter our plans, we are going to the Sandwich Isles in January, returning to Vancouver in March and then, as far as we can tell at present, will remain, here till May, when the flag- ship will relieve us and we will go down to San Francisco, Panama and Valpairaso and other places on the south coast of America, but we cannot count on any certainty in our plans.

"As I write this, we are returning from a cruise in the north of the Island. Amongst other places, we visited Bute Inlet, named after the Isle of Bute in Scotland. Perhaps Uncle Fred knows it, but this is very much grander, the grandest scenery I have ever seen.

The Inlet runs about forty miles into the mainland and in most places, is not more than one and a half miles wide. The shores, on each side, rise precipitously to 5,000, 6,000, or 8,000 feet high, the sides being covered with pines, except where here and there the blasts of winter or the destructive avalanches of early summer have swept away small forests. On entering it, we saw little of the land so close to us, on account of the mists, but later in the day, the hot sun dispelled the clouds and immediately over our heads, the snow-capped mountains burst forth and gave one a regular crick in the neck looking up.

"There is a solemnity in the silence and utter desolation which prevail. Not a living thing disturbs the solitude, the only sound occasionally heard, is the dull roar of the cataract falling into the sea. The whole coast of British Columbia from the Fra-zer River northwards, is indented by similar arms of the sea, not much use as harbours, both on account of their depth and the narrowness which would prevent a sailing ship going up them.
"His next letter described Panama in 1871:

"Panama is a strange-looking old city. It covers a very small portion of ground and is built on a small promontory, having water on three faces of the walls and was, at one time, strongly fortified, the wall being still in existence, though it is broken through in many

Also mentioned in his letter the 1873 visit by the Czarowitch to London who was the heir apparent of the Rus- sian czar. He then goes on to refer to the Royal Tour of In- dia by Prince Albert Edward (Bertie), Queen Victoria's eldest son, 1875 – 76. The 'Edinburgh' he refers to was Queen Victoria's second son Alfred Ernest Albert, Duke of Edinburgh and of Saxe- Coburg- Gotha (August 6, 1844 - 1900) who married Marie Alexander Grand Duchess of Russia (1853 - 1920

parts. It was the headquarters of the old buccaneers and many a land fight they had to defend their city."

"The railway across the Isthmus has its terminus just outside the city. It is very badly managed and is being cut out by the Pacific Rail. The distance from here to

Aspinall, the terminus on the Atlantic side, is only about 45 miles and the train takes 4 hours!

I used to think French trains, at 20 miles an hour, were mighty slow, but this! We are here in almost the worst season, the rainy. This is considered a mild specimen, but it has come in a deluge.

It certainly makes the air cooler, which is a great boon especially as there does not appear to be any 'Doctor', as the sea-breeze is called in most tropical places; where the 'Doctor' comes between 10 and 11 a.m., just when one is beginning to gasp, it continues until the sun's rays are slanting!"

Edward wrote a letter saying they were going to Valparaiso, "nearer you," but they did not return to the south. He wrote once again before returning to England.

"My latest home news came out in the Admiral's bag and is rather old, as it went to China first. The terrible calamity, the foundering of the Captain with nearly 500 on board, is confirmed.

It is the most appalling accident that has occurred in the Navy for many years, only one warrant officer and 17 men saved. The Captain, a V.C., was such a fine fellow.

"Ashley is now on the 'Devastation,' the ship that has been creating a stir, something like the Captain but having no sails, is not considered so dangerous."

Edward's letter from England, at the end of the cruise, contained family news.

It began, *You will be glad to hear of our safe arrival after all that cruising on the briny!*

Was it not odd that the very day I got here, I heard that my brother James, with wife and family were off to Vancouver. I immediately went to London and had 3 or 4 days with him. He has a very good appointment and a nice home to go to. Ashley is on the 'Devastation,' so we appear to be fated to be scattered over the globe.

Our Aunt Maria is well and her husband is as full of fun as ever. He and his son-in-law have just gone for a cruise. Here, in Banbury, they talk of nothing but the Shah, who is staying here, with his diamonds and pink-tailored charger. They rave about him, "but I haven't the curiosity to call.

The Duke of Edinburgh is really engaged at last, to Princess Marie, of Russia, which affair has been much talked of, in England, for the last six months. The Czarowitch and the Czarina have been staying with the Prince of Wales for the last three weeks. You know the two princesses are sisters and I suppose, clinched the affair.

HMS Captain identified by Edward's letter sank on 6 September 1870 off Cape Finisterre, Spain. All 500 on board were lost ncluding Captain Hugh T. Burgoyne, V.C.; Captain Coles, C.B.; This was mainly due to poor design manufacture largely as a result of bureaucratic menace.
Picture HMS Captain William Frederick Mitchell • Public domain

"Croquet has now become a regular science here. They have hoops 4 inches wide, just room for the ball to go through and the mallets are large, flat-faced things which need good muscle to wield. A game of croquet is a serious matter."

Edward's next ship was H.M.S. *Undaunted*, which was ordered to India.

Figure 29 HMS Undaunted Public

I hope this will reach you in time to wish you the Compliments of the Season, as they are called in the Height of Polite Society. A Happy New Year and many of them. I received your letter at Trincomalee be- fore we went to Bombay to receive the Prince of Wales. Since then we have had grand doings and are on the way to Colombo to receive him on his arrival there. Not half as jolly as a Flying Squadron visit to the Australian Colonies which, however, happens only once in a lifetime! We have twelve ships of various sizes under our Admiral's orders to receive H.R.H. and it was rather a fine sight on the morning we arrived, to see them all dressed out with flags and the yards manned. Bombay was full of excitement and of native princes. and rajahs, who were resplendent with jewellery of very barbarous construction, but containing stones of great value. The young Gaekwad of Baroda was raised from the gutter, where he was amusing himself in the manufacture of mud pies, being at the age of 11 or 12, when the lately deposed Gaekwad was deposed for attempting to poison the British Resident, also for misruling his territory. As he stood, he was worth about two million.

He wore a necklace of diamonds of great size, commencing at the back of the neck, with 3 rows expanding in front on the breast into seven rows, with a large one in the centre. The second largest diamond in the world.

Sir Sayaji Rao III, Maharaja of Baroda, 1889 un- known photographer

He used to dress in black velvet, which set the diamonds off, and wore an aigrette of diamonds in his turban. Emeralds also are a favourite decoration, as earrings, bracelets and coronets. In fact, some princes were so covered in emeralds and rubies that it made one suspect that they were nothing but coloured glass, if one were not quite sure to the contrary. This mania for jewelry is in all classes.

I saw a servant with scarcely a shilling of clothes on his back, wearing diamond ear- rings which I would have considered a great bargain for £15.

Of course, there was an immense amount of saluting and I was in full dress uniform for days. No joke in a climate like Bombay in November and still less of a joke to attempt dancing in a buttoned-up tunic and yet people did dance and so did I, considering myself a lunatic all the time! The Prince did a fair amount of dancing considering he is rather corpulent and feels the heat so much, but then he enjoyed the cool garden of the Governor's house, in the pale moonlight and that made the dames of Bombay, whom he did not dance with, abuse the fortunate ones, whom he noticed, as only jealous people can. He made himself popular, as he always does, by his affability and people are quite astonished to find a Prince, who will be a King and who can talk and laugh like an ordinary man.'

There is no doubt that H.R.H. has a very charming manner quite different from Edinburgh, who is reserved and very much on his dignity.

The European part of Bombay has handsome buildings, but the native part is

King's/Queen's Shilling (until 1879) given to new British recruits Dictionary.com sighted 2015 dusty and smelly and so crowded, I wonder how such a handful as we are, kept possession of the country.

His next letter, on his return to England, was from the Royal Barracks, Walmer,

I quite despair of ever hearing from any of the Hobart Town cousins, the date of the last letter is eleven months ago! I must confess to being a bad correspondent, but do not make me worse by dropping me altogether. I think, when I wrote, I was spending my long leave at Banbury on return from foreign service.

After that I was stationed at Plymouth for a few weeks and then was appointed to this place. This is not a regular garrison town, but a dull, quiet seaside town, facing the Goodwin Sands and only at all cheerful for the two or three months in the summer when visitors are here. We have a large recruiting and training establishment where we teach our recruits, before drafting them off to their respective headquarters. We generally have a thousand or so of them going at it all day long, doing "goose step," "shoulder arms," " gymnastics," "schooling" and, in fact, as school circulars say, "all the advantages of a good liberal education, to make them become ornaments to their country. They are all kinds, good, bad or indifferent, some, the very scum of our large towns, up to every kind of villainy, others, men who have received a good education and even gentlemen who have been compelled, thro' the force of circumstances to take the 'Queen's shilling,* but they soon get knocked into shape here, and after six months, their friends would not recognise them

I shall not be sorry when my own tour of duty is done and I can return to my old quarters at Plymouth. The latest excitement in this country is the arrival of the Duke of Edinburgh with his bride. I was fortunate enough to be sent up to London on duty, with the troops lining the streets on the day the Queen brought her up to Windsor and so got a very good view of her. She has a sweet-looking little face, not exactly pretty, perhaps, but very taking. The Queen looked very well and appeared pleased at the bride's reception. The Duke and Princess Beatrice occupied the other two seats in the carriage. The former looked quite handsome and the Princess too, is decidedly pretty.

Unfortunately we had rather a cold day. It snowed the whole time, strange too, wasn't it, that the only bit of winter we have really had, should come on that day. Of course the papers say it was "charmingly appropriate" to a Russian Princess and called the snow storm "the bridal wreath," but my notion of it, after standing three hours or

20 Figure 51 Royal procession of Duke of Edinburgh and Princess Marie Alexandrovna, Grand Duchess, Russia 12 March 1874. (Notice the snow!) Public Domain

more was, that I should have welcomed a bit of sun- shine and would have dispensed with "bridal wreaths". The streets were all a mass of colour, decorated with flags and a sight I was very pleased to have seen in spite of the disagreeable day.

The Royal carriage was kept open the whole time, which is very good of Her Majesty, considering the inclement weather. The illustrations in our papers give a very poor idea of the Duchess. I fancy that she must be short-sighted as that would account for the half-timid sort of look, with which she bowed her acknowledgment to the cheering and waving of handkerchiefs.

Several hundred ships frequently pass here during the day and if the wind is favourable, the docks become quite full and night gives them the appearance of a brilliantly lighted, floating city.

I must close, hoping you are well.

Love to my uncle, aunt and other cousins. Yours affectionately, EDWARD SELBY INNES.

Edward did not come to the Colonies again, but he continued to send family news. He married a charming girl and his three sons followed his profession.

Ships from many Nations

In 1873 Sir Charles Du Cane was still Governor of Tasmania, but went to Sydney on a visit and from there wrote, you will probably know that I received a telegram yesterday from Sir George Bowen (first Governor of Queensland), informing me that the 'Garibaldi' is certain not to arrive at Hobart before the 16th. I hope to get back early myself in the same day and I have telegraphed my hope that the Duke of Genoa, with the three na-val officers who compose his suite, will be my guests at Government House during the 'Garibaldi's stay. For how long, I do not know, but the young Duke will take the opportunity to see a little of the colony, as he appears to be doing in Victoria.

"The remains of Mr. Wentworth (which were, as near as possible being thrown overboard on the voyage from England), are at this moment being conveyed to their final resting-place, with much solemnity and Sydney is wearing a—half funeral, half- holiday aspect.

So, though Hobart girls had to lose their friends in the R.N., they were not with- out excitement. Not only Italian but Russian ships came to call and be entertained and flirtations nourished! The Russians particularly wasted no time. In a few days one of their officers all gold braid and buttons called on Mr. Innes. Only two young daughters were at home and he immediately requested one to leave the room, "For," he said, "I wish to ask Miss M. to be my wife!" Both objected one because she wanted to see how he would propose and the other "Because," she said, "do you look for a new wife at every port?" and then offended him by going off into fits of giggles, so that he left. pockets for them.

Elizabeth's penchant for intellectual stimulus and the social life of the colony remained with her forever as shown by this delightful engagement with James Backhouse Walker in the 12th March 1890. 'I took old Mrs. Innes to supper. We just missed the first lot for supper, & had to wait in the passage so long that it was nearly an hour before we got down again. Eve- rybody chaffed me about my very marked flirtation with the old lady.' Letters from Hobart, 1889-1892 : JB Walker to his sister Mary in London / edited & annotated by Margaret Glover p144

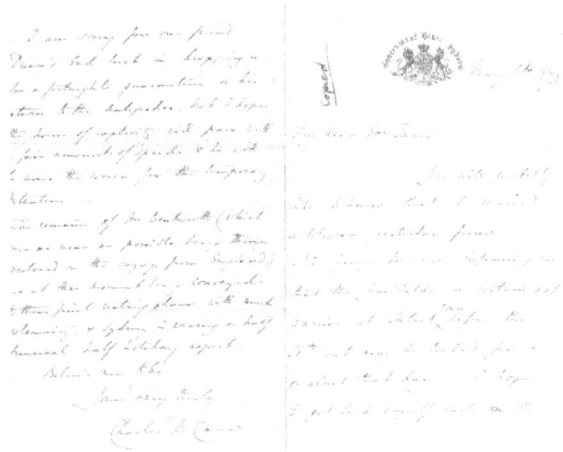

Figure 31 Garabaldi in Bay of Naples Public Domain

Figure 32 Russian warships visit Hobart, 1882: the Afric, Plastown and Vestric (AOT, PH30/1/1809)

About this time F. M. Innes and other politicians visited Port Arthur. Of course there was a great deal there to sadden people, but he came home with an amusing little story. Two or three old "lags" had been deputed to draw the tram in which they travelled across the Peninsula. They had gone about half- way when the tram stopped and the "lags" with one accord, yelled "Baccy, baccy." (tobacco) At first the politicians could hardly believe their ears, then the funny side of it struck them. "Blackmail" from the old chaps, who really hadn't a chance! They had a good laugh and good- humouredy emptied their pockets for them

In 1872 F. Maitland Innes was both Premier and Colonial Treasurer and his old school-friend, J. R. Scott,* was Colonial Secretary.

After Sir Charles Du Cane, Mr. Frederick Weld became Governor. He and his wife were very fond of riding and all out-of-door occupations. They frequently sent notes to *Newlands* asking the Inneses to accom- pany them. On note paper edged with at least an inch of deep black and the coat-of- arms to match (the Court was still in mourning for the Prince Consort). A note would arrive:

"My Dear Mr. Innes,
"After Ex Council to-day, I am driving out to Elwick, probably there may be one or two others, five or six all included, at most. As it is impromptu, I shall basket with something to eat. I wish you would come and I promise to get you back to the Ex. Council in time." Though belonging to one of the greatest families in England, Sir Frederick was not at all formal and he and his wife were most friendly. Like the other Governors and their wives, they often came to 'Newlands' to enjoy and discuss poetry and prose and were most considerate. Knowing that there was no carriage,

though there were always riding horses there, they often ac- companied an invitation to dinner with the offer of the use of a spare carriage.

"Aunt Maria," Frederick's sister whom he had not seen for many years, amused

him with her letters, full of family news, expressed in the verbose manner of the day.

My Dear Frederick,

Can you, amongst your multitudinous and arduous duties, find time to read a screed from me? I have had my paper before me, once or twice, for the purpose of writing, but have been prevented.

I am now in difficulties, snow and sleet are falling, a piercing east wind, the last bitter blast of winter, all these make me shiver and shake and then, to add to this misery, a colliery famine through the coal strike. Coal, formerly 17/-, is now 34/- a ton, is to be got only with difficulty. I do not know what we are coming to, but we do not think it is all a labourer's question.

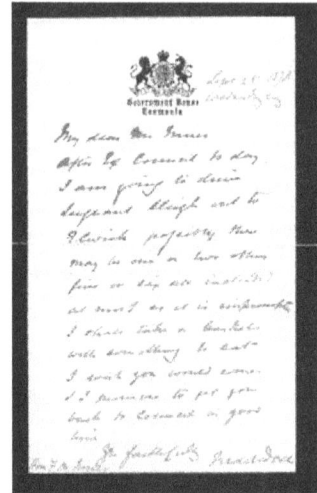

The pit owners are glad of the strike, in as much as the stock of coal is doubled in value and will never again be as low. The ministerial crisis has just taken place, the Ultra More taxes have upset Gladstone's Ministry* and a dis- solution is quite expected.

Our Member, very satisfied, I assume, is, and has been cruising in his own yacht, the "Brilliant," all this winter, in the Mediterranean, having paired off, as he thought, until Easter. Now he must haste home, but I expect you read all about that in the papers, so I will give you all family news.

Your nephew, James, has received the appointment of Chief Naval Storekeeper, at Esquimalt and Francisco. (He later became Governor of Vancouver). His wife (No. 2) and 7 children sail this month to their home.

We all like James, a jolly open-hearted fellow and his wife is excellent, but, alas, too fruitful. Twins in succession, an awful catastrophe! This may be un-objectionable in a colony, but here it is monstrous! My daughter, Jane, and her mother-in-law are going, next week, to a family parting dinner in London. Your sister is not strong enough to travel in winter, so James is coming to wish me farewell. He has a good salary and house and liberal allowances for passages. Edward, whom you have seen, comes home this month, on

H.M.S. 'Scylla.' Poor fellow, he has just heard of his father's

Figure 33 HMS Devastation

(Capt. Henry, R.N.) death, from newspapers at Rio. Ashley is on H.M.S. "Devastation", on a trial trip to Lisbon. She is an odd- looking vessel and looks unsafe, as the " H.M.S Captain" At Plymouth a month before she went down, I told two of her officers, who were not in her, that I thought that would be her fate. He is engaged to a very nice girl of our acquaintance.

She then spoke of others, also of her own delicate health saying too, "I was glad to be near Henry before his death, to cheer   him. Verily, we are all going the same way. How soon?" Your affectionate sister, MARIA.

Maria, in Scotland, and her eldest brother Francis James, were destined to die on the same day, the 18th May, some years later.

Aunt Maria's letter provides some de- lightful insight into the trials and tribulations of life back in
Mother England. She mentions coals strikes which were a fairlycommon oc- currence during this period in England. *The Making of Wigan* By Mike Fletcher 2005 pages75 – 78 Publisher: Wharn- cliffe Books provides a good summary of the subject.
*Gladstone's Ministry refers to William Gladstone (29/12/1808 – 19/5/1898) who was Britain's longest serving PM

The Parson

One member of the Grey family who was not a fighting man George Basil Anderson, died on 11 July 1896. The journalist writing his obituary notice rose to such heights that it is worth quoting. (His mother was Sarah Grey.)

The quaint town of Dingle has been thrown into profound grief since the news of the death of the Protestant Rector of the Parish became known at

1.30 on last Saturday afternoon. Though Mr. Anderson has been suffering from rheumatic gout for some time past his death was unexpected. Never has there been signs of a more thorough and genuine sorrow felt on all sides, than that brought about by the sudden demise of this most popular person.

> The Parson
> George Basil Anderson (mother Jane Margaret Catherine Gray b 1810) Clerke in Holy Or- ders, Chaplin in
> H.M Ecclesiastical Estab- lishment of India, Kotree Scinde (possibly Kotri Sindh). 1865 – 68. Hydrabad (Hyderabad) and Kotree (Kotri) 1868 – 73 and later Rector of Dingle, County Kerry – Ireland for 19 years. b Jan 1835 d 1896 aged 61 unmarried. (FNB)

He was respected and admired by the Lord in his Mansion, he was loved and adored by the fisher boy on the pier.

The Parish Priest spoke in flattering terms of him and his Curates (the priests) walked side by side with him. The country farmers took off their hats in humble but sincere respect for the Parson, whilst the passing tourists called and came away deeply impressed with the brilliant conversation of the Rector of Dingle. The poor Roman Catholic, going his way received as much kindness at his hands as did his Protestant brother. Mr. Anderson was endowed with remarkable talents, and being so, was much esteemed by men holding very influential positions in London and Dublin. When in India as Army Chaplain, with the Colonel of the Regiment, as well as the Hindoo servant, he was always a recognised favourite, always humming, always whistling, ever ready to brighten society with a story of real life. He endeared himself to all. He was a refined entertainer, a wonderful reader of character, a brilliant and interesting conversationalist, possessing noble principles and a heart as big as Connor Hill.x

The Parson, as he was always called with reverence and affection, was ever ready, anxious and willing to render assistance to the poor boy about to embark on this world's voyage. His kind advice and tuition had been given freely to the school lad, possessing an ambition to succeed and make a name for himself in life, and those who had been guided by him, and they are many, to-day occupy social positions of good standing. His talents were of a most versatile character. He was a tenor vocalist of much sweetness, an instrumentalist of no mean order, and a painter if he devoted enough attention to its study, should have executed some commendable work.

He was a severe but impartial critic, a profound scholar mathematically, classically, and scientifically. Why such a distinguished character preferred to live in a lovely village by the sea, away from the society to which he had been accustomed, previous to his taking the rector-ship, I have no answer.

His mother, to whom he was devoted lived with him, but died suddenly some years ago, and his spirits never seemed the same. His sermons were of a practical kind, extempore and well-pointed. He neither had nor professed any better object in his career than to do good to others. He was a genuine, a great and kind man, a noble friend and great companion. As a student of Trinity College, Dublin, he distinguished himself. He was proud of his county, Kilkenny, a thorough Church of Ireland Clergyman, he loved the sim- ple form of worship. Fond of youth, fishing, driving and boating, the dear Parson was a familiar figure with the boys going to and from school, as well as with the big guns in the musical and theatrical professions in London and Dublin.

He was an actor of ability. I have been associated with him from childhood. I cherished his society, appreciated his teaching and my grief at his death is great. I have lost the greatest of my friends.

William D'Arcey, London.

At his funeral, an oak coffin, covered with flowers, was carried from his home to his church on the shoulders of coastguards, police men and civilians who relieved each other. The internment took place in the cemetery of Raheenanwhing. Many clergy of many denominations, all the inhabitants of Dingle and many from Tralee were present, evidence of the deep feeling of the loss sustained by people of all classes and creeds.

All business places and banks were closed. The Sessions Court was adjourned, the chairman of the Sessions said, "I wish to adjourn this court for the day. We feel a public loss has been sustained. We Catholics showed at his funeral how greatly we feel it," and finished, "He bore without abuse, the grand old name of gentleman.

The late Rector had been Clerk in Holy Orders, Chaplain in H.M. Ecclesiastical Establishment in India, Kotree Slinde, and later Hyderabad and Kotree before he settled in Ireland. Evidently the Rector had learnt to make mind triumph over matter, as his gout did not prevent his boating or fishing!

Later Generations

Elizabeth and Frederick had some happy years, until as President of the Legislative Council, he went to Launceston, contracted pneumonia and passed away in 1882. All the papers contained long columns of laudatory obituary no- tices and later, Major Fenton, in his history summed them up, saying, "The Hon. F.M. Innes took an active part in leading questions, was a ready writer and an eloquent speaker. His loss was much regretted in educational circles and privately, by a great number of friends."

His daughter, Catherine Henrietta, married George Hamilton Dougharty of Innesowen, N.S.W. [on 23rd May 1874. They had seven children: Jean, Frederick, Kate author of this book, George, Isabel, Ethel and Douglas.]

Catherine Henrietta Innes born At Newtown Hobart V D Land 19th November 1844 at ½ to 5 AM
(Source Sarah Elizabeth Innes bible)

"Traist" [Be Faithful] is the [Innes] family motto. Their eldest son Frederick gave his life for his country [on 23rd April 1818] and was buried in [METEREN

MILITARY CEMETERY] Northern France, where he lies, with many of his fellow Britons from all over the Dominions.

On the road by the cemetery the French erected a monument on which they carved:

Here the invaders did not pass. His young brother Douglas was in France with the Army Field Ambulance and returned safely. Their cousins, too young to be married, are buried in Gallipoli and France.* In World War II, Catherine's very young, and only grandson, Geoffrey Ashton-Jones, begged until he had his parents' consent to go overseas and after fighting with the 2nd A.I.F in El Alamein, Syria, Egypt, New Guinea and Borneo, came home exhausted, but happy.

Douglas Hamilton Dougharty enlisted in C Section 2nd Field Ambulance A.I. for active service 1915. Served in France 1916 & 1917 at Ypres, Armentieres, Poper- ingle (Belgium) Albert, Amiens, the battle of Bullecourt. See East Melbourne Historical Society website for more information.

Figure 57 From Australian War Memorial

---

*One such cousin William Maitland Innes, was wounded in the head but as a less severe case than others offered to wait bandaged and waited three days for attention – saying "100 Turks won't kill me" They got him to the hospital ship, but seeing another Australian, wounded, unconscious and stripped – William crawled off the ship along the terrible beach and bought him safely to the ship. This man lived to thank William's father and raised a memorial to him. William died of his wounds 17th May 1915 aged 22 and is buried in Egypt. (FNB)

Finally the old Innes history concluded.

"In all which long tract of tyme, there are three things wherein they are notable or happy, as they themselves say. First that their inheritance never went to a woman, Second, that none of them ever married an ill wife;

Thirdly, that no friend every suffered for their debt. Whether this be true or not, I know not, but if it be, let them be more thankful to the Lord for His goodness, who has continued them, so long, without reproach and you can yet add to their succession, if they be humble before him and honest towards man. But if they be vain and misimprove the kyndness of God, how easily can He put a period to their race and cast them out of His sight, as He dayly doth, with many greater and better than they."

The Greys and their descendants were true Britons, as Winston Churchill described them, "The spirit of an unconquerable people, a spirit lived in freedom, nursed in tradition, which has come down to us through the centuries."

An Early Victorian Poem - Written by One of the Family

Only two old shabby volumes in torn lids of dusty green, With some frayed and faded markers, laid the time-worn leaves between,

But full many a heaven-sent lesson have their pages to me taught, Breathing sweetly words of comfort to sore heart and brain o'er- wrought,

Calmly now, in life's grey autumn, I can read them once again, Stormy passion long since vanished, peace outweighing all the pain, But a tear will start at seeing a beloved familiar word,

And the ear is almost listening for a voice no longer heard.

I can ne'er forget the summer, when they first were given to me, And the dear delight of reading, in the giver's company,

Or when some sweet passage touched us, seeming writ to us alone; How his lines crept up the margin, very faint and pale now grown, Ah, the dear dead hand that traced, lies beneath the daisies now,

But each mark recalls the expression of his eye his lips and brow And I ask that these old volumes may my last low pillow

be, Like my own, their mission ended, let them fall to dust with me.

An Early Victorian Poem

This poem also appears in a book by Andrew Kennedy Hutchison Boyd (2013). pp. 280-1. *Twenty-Five Years of St.*
Andrews, September 1865 to *September, 1890* (Vol. 5). London: Forgotten Books. (Original work published 1892)
He writes as follows
*Just on May 12, 1887, a specially hearty letter came from far away in Devonshire, sending a little volume of very pleasing verses. I had quite forgot the little book, till it became needful to read that old history. But I really must give some lines from a poem entitled * St. John xiii. 7.' The passage of scripture is strong reason. 'What I do thou knowest not now; but thou shalt know hereafter.' Only two old shabby volumes, in torn lids of dusky green, With some frayed and faded markers, laid the time-worn leaves between* : Followed by the full poem.

This completes the work by Kate Dougharty

www.ingramcontent.com/pod-product-compliance
Lightning Source LLC
Chambersburg PA
CBHW080858090426
42738CB00014B/3195